With
Long Life

Southern Publishing Association, Nashville, Tennessee

With Long Life
Penny Estes Wheeler

Copyright © 1978 by
Southern Publishing Association

This book was
Edited by Richard Coffen
Designed by Mark O'Connor
Cover painting by Phil Crowe

Type set: 10/12 Melior

Printed in U.S.A.

Library of Congress Cataloging in Publication Data

Wheeler, Penny Estes.
  With long life.

    SUMMARY: Fourteen stories illustrating Seventh-day Adventist principles.
  I. Title.
PZ7.W5664Wi   78-13748
ISBN 0-8127-0192-5

Dedicated

to my father, James Estes,
who knew Tucker Webb,
to my uncle, Bob Prestridge,
Annie's big brother,
and
to my friend
Mr. Hugh Smith.

Contents

"With Long Life"	11
Tucker Webb's Christmas	23
A Quilt of Comfort	31
The Silent Customer	45
The Recluse	53
Thunderstorm	61
The Lounger	65
The Secret	71
Wild Horse	77
Gift of Love	87
Weekend of Terror	95
Right Angles and a Prayer	107
The Ungrateful Cow	113
Stalled	119

Lisey flopped onto a chair, her long legs dangling over the side. "Grandma," she wailed, "there's nothing to do."

Her grandmother nudged her glasses up and snapped off a thread from the red material in her lap. "School hasn't been out a week, and already you've got nothing to do?"

"Well, Peg's cleaning people's houses, and she's promised maybe to help me find some work, too, but she worked last summer and doesn't have to worry. Besides, she's older." Lisey frowned. "No one wants a fourteen-year-old with no experience."

"No baby-sitting?"

"Simon tonight. He's easy. But I've got this whole afternoon and—" she shrugged. "I'll probably go bananas before school starts again."

Grandmother put aside her sewing for a moment. "I'll tell you what. I've got a stack of hemming and handwork to do this afternoon. You sit here and help me, and I'll practice the story I'm going to tell in the junior department Sabbath."

Lisey brightened. "I didn't know you had a story there this week. What's it about?"

"You get started slip-stitching this neck facing, and I'll tell you," her grandmother smiled.

Chapter 1

"With Long Life"

The night wind moaned softly through the deep forest surrounding the small white house. Suddenly a noise different from the muted night sounds awakened Mrs. Paulson. Her body tensed as she half sat up to listen. Glancing down, she saw that little Betsy slept soundly in the trundle bed beside her. "Perhaps the cow's gotten out," she mused, "or maybe the door latch is loose. I wish Karl didn't have to work away from home," she thought as she got up to investigate.

She did not bother to light a lamp as she padded her way through the dark house, pausing momentarily to check the sleeping forms of Karl, Jr., and Sara in the next room. As she opened the front door she pulled her robe closer against the night chill, then went down the three steps into the yard. A full moon's cloud-filtered rays filled the small clearing and outlined the toolshed and water pump with a strange, shimmering light.

Mrs. Paulson listened in the darkness. No sound. The cow was sleeping peacefully in her shed, and the chickens were quiet in their coop. The wind sigh-sighed through the trees and caused the wild flowers to nod gently in the dappled moonlight.

"A lonely sound, the wind," Mother Paulson thought. "Especially now with Karl having just left for a week away from home." But a woodcutter can't make a living unless he can sell his wood, she knew, so her husband had taken his boards to a cabinet shop in the city fifty miles away.

She stood a moment longer, enjoying the moonlit beauty. Then, deciding that she had probably heard some small night animal, or nothing at all, she turned to go back inside to bed. For a moment she paused in front of the doorway. Her bare foot rested for only an instant on something both solid, yet soft, before she jerked it back. But it was enough for her to feel a sharp stab on her ankle. A second later the long body of a snake undulated through the grass and into the protective blackness of the woods.

Terror-filled, Mrs. Paulson hurried into the house. With trembling fingers she lit a lamp, then lifted her long robe to examine the double pinprick on her ankle. Already the skin around it felt tender. Sinking into a chair, she sat quietly, waiting for her mind to grasp the reality that she knew but could not accept: Tomorrow at this time she would probably be dead.

"Could it have been less than twenty-four hours since Karl left?" she wondered numbly. She didn't even have to close her eyes to see him riding away on the trail through the woods, his red shirt flashing patches of color even after the thickset trees had swallowed him from view.

"You're the man of the family while I'm gone," the father had told his namesake.

And Karl, Jr., just turned thirteen, had nodded solemnly and said, "Yes, sir, I'll take care of our three ladies."

Holding baby Betsy, who chortled with delight, Mr. Paulson had kissed ten-year-old Sara good-bye and tousled her red hair. Then, untangling Betsy's fingers from his beard, he gave her to his wife, whom he kissed

"With Long Life" 13

again, and left. "See you in a week," he called.

The pain in her ankle brought Mrs. Paulson back to the present. "What will I do with the children?" she thought wildly. "We have no neighbors. No one comes by. There's not even another horse for Karl to ride and find aid. . . . Help me, Lord," she prayed. "If You see fit to let me die, show me how to keep my children safe and well until their father comes home." She squeezed her eyes shut, and tears fell down her cheeks. "But I don't want to die, dear Father," she added. "If there's any way, . . . don't let me die."

Mrs. Paulson stood up, took the lamp, and walked slowly into the kitchen, knowing what she had to do.

First the fire. She worked with the banked coals in the oven until they blazed merrily. Moving quietly so she wouldn't awaken the children, she filled two pots with water. Into one she put dried pinto beans—lima beans into the other—and placed both on the stove to cook. Then she set the yeast sponge for a double recipe of bread. Sitting at the table to rest a moment, her fingers caressed the flour-sack cloth. She'd been proud when she had finished the tablecloth, first bleaching it in the sunlight, then dyeing it with the juice of wild berries.

Her fingers touched the burning pain in her lower leg. "I'm helpless," she thought, angry with herself. "I don't even know what to do to counteract the snake's poison. Granny would have known what to do—or my mother, or Aunt Freda. All I can do here is sit and wait.

"Enough food to last a week," she told herself. "I've got to fix sufficient food for the week. And most of the children's clothes are dirty, too. I must wash Betsy's diapers, though that will be all I'll be able to do. Karl and Sara can help with the cooking and washing. Oh, but I wish they'd sleep late today. How I dread trying to explain to them. They'll be so frightened."

Pushing against the top of the table, she got up to stir the beans, to add an onion to the pintos, and to knead the bread. By the time the sunlight awakened the children, the first loaves of golden baking bread filled the little house with their fragrance.

"Hi, Mom. What are you baking so early for?" Karl asked, rubbing his eyes as he entered the kitchen.

"We havin' company or something?" Sara added as she came in behind her brother.

Their mother managed to smile, thinking it was good that her robe hid her swelling leg. "I couldn't sleep, so thought I'd catch up on my baking." The baby awoke and began to cry. "Sara, honey, please bring Betsy in here so I can feed her."

The infant finished nursing just as Karl, with a pail of milk, walked into the kitchen. He strained it through two white cloths and then went to the pantry for the big pot in which to boil it. "Mom, I can't find the milk pot," he called.

Mrs. Paulson, who was now in the back bedroom dressing Betsy, replied, "I guess I'm cooking beans in it. Just a minute, and I'll see what I can find." Slowly, painfully, she hobbled the few steps to the kitchen. "Let's use two smaller ones," she said. She checked the bread, took the loaves from the oven, spread the crust with fresh butter, and laid a clean cloth over them.

"I'm going to get dressed," she told her son, "then we'll have breakfast." She dressed hurriedly but carefully, choosing a blue-sprigged print that she usually saved for trips to town. "The extra-full ruffled skirt will hide my leg," she told herself while coiling her long hair and pinning it up. Pausing for a peek in the old, battered mirror, she straightened her turned-up collar.

"How about an old-fashioned breakfast?" she asked Karl and Sara after returning to the kitchen.

"You mean no biscuits or pancakes?" Sara answered.

"When I was a very little girl and Mamma was in a hurry, this was the breakfast we always had. Mamma said she liked it best of all. Sara, go down to the cellar and bring up a jar of peaches. That will be like dessert with our bread and milk."

Karl set the table while his mother broke thick hunks of almost-stale whole-wheat bread and poured cold, creamy milk over them. Sara came up with the peaches and stopped to impulsively hug her mother. "I really like your old-fashioned breakfast," she said. "I can pretend I'm a pioneer like Grandma was."

Before they sat down, Mrs. Paulson got the little padded stool to prop her leg on as she ate. Although she tried to do it while the children were busy, Karl saw her adjusting her foot to a comfortable position and asked if she'd hurt her leg. Shrugging off the question without answering, she bowed her head to thank God for the food. Karl's inquiry vanished in Sara's chatter about how many eggs she might find that morning and in Betsy's happy squeal. The boy brought the baby to the table for his mother to hold while they ate.

"Would you please clear the table, Sara?" Mrs. Paulson directed, "and Karl, bring me the Bible." She lingered over worship as long as she dared. The pain in her leg was increasing, and she knew that she had a week's work to do in the next few hours. Closing the Bible, she looked at her children, swallowed hard, and chose her words carefully.

"I've been bitten... by a snake," she began, trying to keep her voice even. "On my ankle." She talked on, desperately attempting to think of some way to erase the fright in the faces before her. "My leg is swelling already from the poison, and unless a miracle happens, pretty soon I must lie down and go to sleep."

"No, Mamma. *No!*" Sara cried. The freckles on her white face stood out like brown buttons. Racing to her mother, she buried her face in her hair.

Karl looked squarely at his mother, his large brown eyes unblinking, unbelieving. "A doctor," he managed. "I'll go for the doctor."

"With no horse, my son, and no neighbors to borrow one from or to tell?" As she spoke softly, gently, she caressed Sara's hair with one hand and held Betsy tightly with the other. "The problem is caring for you children until Father comes. You must be brave. You must help me prepare food, enough food to last all week. And Betsy must have clean diapers. You two, my little man and woman, must take care of each other and of Betsy until Father comes home." She swallowed hard to keep from choking on her words. "Don't be afraid for me. Jesus will awaken me when the time comes. But I must know that you can care for each other and for Betsy."

Karl returned her look, strong and brave, while large tears poured down his cheeks. "We'll be all right, Mamma. I promised Dad I'd take care of you and Sara and Betsy, and I'll do everything I can."

His mother reached across the table to put her hand over his clenched fists. "Let's pray before we begin our day."

After prayer, Karl brought water, and he and Sara washed Betsy's diapers and a few of their clothes while their mother finished the second batch of bread. Sara brought potatoes from the cellar, which Mother boiled. She also managed to churn some butter and hard-boil the eggs that Sara gathered. Still, she worried that her children wouldn't have enough food.

By noon, Mrs. Paulson couldn't stand up any longer; so she sat on a couch, her bright-blue ruffled skirt hiding

"With Long Life" 17

her leg which had now swollen to twice its size. Sara brought some paper and a pen, and her mother wrote a letter to her husband and directions for the children: how to cook dandelion greens, how to chop the boiled potatoes with onions and fry them in the skillet, how to cream the potatoes, how to make soup from the scraps.

Under her mother's instructions, Sara mixed up a formula for Betsy to drink and tried to feed the baby from a cup. The girl cried as the infant resisted her efforts, but Mother assured her that she'd learn quickly. "If all else fails," Mrs. Paulson said, blinking back her own tears, "dip the twisted edge of a clean cloth into the milk and let Betsy suck on that. You might crumble up some bread and add milk and feed her that with a spoon."

She motioned to the Bible that still lay on the kitchen table. "Read to each other, will you?" she said. "Don't forget to have worship every morning and night. The Psalms are nice for children to read, and of course the Four Gospels. They'll keep you company while you're waiting for Father."

Mrs. Paulson had Karl take the baby's little bed into the two older children's room. Sara followed with Betsy's clothes and blankets. "After I'm . . . asleep, keep my door closed," their mother told them. "That way you won't have so much house to keep warm on cool nights. And be sure to keep booties on Betsy so she won't catch cold or get colic."

Mother rocked Betsy to sleep while the other two children hurried around, following her directions for storing the food she had prepared. Karl put the baby to bed, then returned to the kitchen where his mother sat writing again. Her leg was propped up on a chair. "Don't you want to lie down?" he asked.

"Not yet, not yet. The kitchen is cheery, and I like to be where I can see and hear you two."

Several miles away Mr. Hamilton and his Indian wife were returning to their farm after a day in town. They'd gotten up before the sun, done a day's work before breakfast, then hurried into town for their monthly shopping. Now, as they rode in their wagon loaded with purchases, Mr. Hamilton loosely held the reins and let the horse take them home at its own leisurely trot.

The midafternoon sun warmed them, even through the shadows cast by the trees on both sides of the road. Violets, clustered among heart-shaped leaves, nestled against the roots of the trees. "Katherine Paulson's favorite, she always said," Mrs. Hamilton commented. "You know she lives just a couple of miles down the next road we're coming to."

"Does she?" came her husband's tired reply.

"Let's run by and see her. It's been months, what with winter and all that late snow we had."

"We'll have to hurry to beat sundown as it is," Mr. Hamilton answered as the horse trotted past the road that went to the Paulson house.

His wife put her hand on his arm. "Please, Henry. Wouldn't take but an hour to stop by and say hello. Her husband works away from home, you know, and she gets lonesome for company. She has a new baby that I've only seen once."

"Well——"

"Katherine was always a good friend to me. Remember when I was sick and she sent that crock of beans and sweet cake to help out while I couldn't cook?"

"I know when I'm licked," Mr. Hamilton grouched good-naturedly, turning the horse around and urging him to trot faster.

The sun had already hidden behind the trees as the Hamiltons drove into the Paulson yard. Sara saw them first. "Mamma! Mamma! Karl! Somebody's comin'!" she shrieked, racing to where her mother lay.

Karl raced out the door. "My mom—she's awful sick," he cried.

Without waiting for her husband to help her, Mrs. Hamilton gathered up her full skirt, jumped from the wagon, and hurried into the house. "Katherine, what is it?" she gasped, taking in the food-laden kitchen, Sara's frightened face, and her friend's pale, sad one.

"Early this morning, before dawn, a snake bit me on the ankle." Mrs. Paulson slowly labored over each word.

Mrs. Hamilton lifted Katherine's skirt and saw the grotesquely enlarged limb, streaked and discolored from the poison. "Henry!" she called. "Children! Help me. Come out to the woods."

Under her direction they began searching for a betony vine that grew wild among the trees. When they'd gathered an armload, she and her husband went back to the house while Sara and Karl stayed behind to collect more. Mrs. Hamilton helped her friend into bed while Mr. Hamilton set a pot of water on the stove to heat. Then she instructed her husband to chew the leaves into a mulch, spit them out, and chew some more. She did the same, and within minutes Mrs. Hamilton had packed the crushed leaves around part of the swollen leg and had rushed outside for more.

"We've got to get the leg covered, and chewing is the fastest way," she explained to her husband. "Once it's covered good, we'll boil some to a paste and pack that around her leg."

The man shook his head. "It seems hopeless," he whispered.

"God can work miracles, and sometimes we can help Him," his wife replied. "I've seen this help before"—she frowned a second—"but never on a person so far gone." She hurried through the woods and with flying fingers stripped leaves from the vines that hugged the trees. She puffed to her husband, "I guess I'm the only person around these parts except maybe the doctor who'd know what to do. And even Doc might not know about these leaves drawing out the poison."

Mrs. Paulson moaned, hardly conscious of the activity around her. Betsy cried and Sara tried to comfort her, tried to feed her, and finally put her back into bed so she could gather leaves with her brother and Mr. Hamilton. The man lit a lamp, and they worked far into the night. Mrs. Hamilton applied fresh, hot poultices as fast as her husband and the children could keep her supplied. "Thank God the plants are close by," she told her husband as he brought in another basket of leaves.

Sara and Karl refused to stop working and go to bed, even though sometime past midnight Mrs. Hamilton urged them to do so. The children did stop long enough to tiptoe into their mother's room and watch as the woman changed the poultice. Slowly, almost imperceptibly, yet surely, the swelling began to go down and the redness to fade from the misshapen leg. By dawn the children fell exhausted into their beds. Mr. Hamilton slipped some buttered bread into his pocket and left in the wagon to find more leaves.

Betsy cried, and Sara, tossing in a restless sleep, didn't hear. But the sound pierced into their mother's room. A shaft of sunlight fell across her face. She opened her eyes, slowly, remembering something that she wanted to forget. Shaking her aching head, she tried to focus her eyes upon someone leaning above her. "Fairlight Hamilton?" she whispered, unbelieving. And then, "Am I still . . . alive?"

Mrs. Hamilton's dark braid had loosened around her face. She pushed the hair back from her eyes with a work-stained hand. "Not only alive, but"—and her smile was that of an angel—"I believe you're going to keep right on living!"

Mr. Hamilton returned with more leaves. When he left again, he went for the doctor. After Mrs. Hamilton applied the new poultice, she asked if her friend wanted anything.

"A swallow of water, and if you're not too tired—and oh, I'm sure you're tired—would you get the Bible and read Psalm 91 to me?" Mrs. Paulson whispered.

The soft voice of Mrs. Hamilton sounded like an angel's song to her, even if the woman did stumble over some of the words. " 'He shall call upon me, and I will answer him,' " she read. " 'I will be with him in trouble; I will deliver him, and honour him.' " She paused to smile at Katherine Paulson before finishing the final verse. " 'With long life will I satisfy him, and shew him my salvation.' "

June bugs sang as Lisey and her family sat on their wide front porch in the early June evening. They talked quietly and watched the scant traffic pass by.

"Uncle Bob told me a sad thing this morning," Lisey ventured.

"He's lonely," Mother observed. "It's nice you go talk to him."

"Oh, I like to talk to him. Besides, I've got more time than I know what to do with these days."

"No luck with Peggy's job leads?" her father asked.

"Yes." Lisey stopped rocking to talk. "In fact, tomorrow I'm going to baby-sit with Mrs. Appel's six-month-old and do a little cleaning for her from ten to two."

"How much will she pay?" Mother asked.

Lisey frowned. "She didn't say."

"Oh, well," Grandmother put in, "at least you're

getting experience. Once people know you want to clean and baby-sit, you'll have more work than you can handle."

"I hope," the girl sighed.

Suddenly a blue jay dive-bombed a cat that wandered too near its nest, and they all laughed.

"What did you start to say about Uncle Bob?" Mother chuckled.

"His little sister, Annie."

"Oh, yes." And they were all silent for a moment, remembering.

"I've got a story for you," Dad broke the quiet. "It's a happy one, Lisey. Did I ever tell you about Tucker Webb?"

"Who?"

"Tucker Webb. Lived in Mesquite a hundred years ago when I was a little boy."

"A hundred years, Daddy?"

"Well—at least fifty. He was a cripple and sort of the town fixture."

"Tell her about Christmas," Mother prompted. "That's always my favorite."

"OK. You all get settled. This is rather long."

"We're settled."

Dad sat quietly for a minute or so, his mind reaching back some fifty-five years. Back beyond satellites and 707s, past CBs and electric can openers. Back to a windswept Texas town the week before Christmas . . .

Chapter 2

Tucker Webb's Christmas

The Texas wind blew cold that morning before Christmas, and I pulled the patchwork quilt tightly around me, making myself a warm island in the icy bed.

Christmas Eve.

I sighed, shivering against the prairie wind that moaned around the windows and whistled into the room. Christmas was for little children. At least that's what Auntie said. But Dad didn't think so. And tonight . . .

At twelve years of age, I'd stretched up tall and gangling. Suddenly my overalls were too short for my legs, and my bony wrists hung well below the cuffs of my plaid flannel shirts. My voice played tricks on me. And my hair grew dark and thick, spilling out from under my cap in an unruly way that annoyed my aunt.

I lived with my aunt, uncle, and cousins—had ever since my mother died. Since I hardly remembered Mamma, I didn't miss her much. My dad was a building contractor, constructing houses for others and always sorry that he couldn't give me a home. He worked in Fort Worth. Quite a city. A hundred times bigger than Mesquite.

But he'd be coming tonight, arriving about nine o'clock on the Texas and Pacific and bringing Christmas with him.

We didn't have a tree. Almost nobody did. They didn't bring trees in by the thousands from Michigan and Canada like they do today. Oh, some families might go out and cut down a cedar tree, but it was usually small and sticky and lopsided.

The church would have one, though. The members scouted all over the county until they found a good-sized cedar. Then the children made paper chains, and the ladies' club strung popcorn to wind around it. No electricity ran to the church yet, and of course candles were too dangerous, so the popcorn and chains were about all the decorations it had.

The town was different too. Different, I mean, from the way they look nowadays around Christmastime. No tinsel hung from the streetlights, no plastic Santas winked from store windows, and the dry goods store didn't have "Silent Night" and "Here Comes Santa Claus" piped in over an intercom to inspire shoppers to buy more.

Not that we didn't have a pretty little town. Built on the Texas flatlands, the stores and offices stood impressively around the grassy square. Summertimes we could pitch horseshoes there. Mesquite was a real nice town, as towns went in the early 1920s. The stores weren't crowded with Christmas bargains as they are today— just a few simple toys like dolls or trains or balls were about all one could find. Actually it didn't matter. The farmers and just about everybody else had little money to spend anyway.

Auntie and Uncle Charlie didn't buy presents now that we weren't little kids anymore. But in a few hours Dad would arrive, suitcases filled with white tissue-wrapped packages for all of us, plus sacks of fruit and hard candy.

The day dragged by. Feed the cows, milk the cows,

Tucker Webb's Christmas

eat breakfast, chop the wood, bring in the wood, help Uncle in the barn, assist Auntie around the house. At last we finished supper, and Uncle Charlie went out to start the old 490 Chevy. I felt proud to ride in the car and profoundly thankful that we hadn't had rain to make the dirt roads into ribbons of mud. If it had rained, we'd have had to take the buggy or wagon, and thirty degrees with a hard wind made it much too cold for that.

My cousin Bud and I climbed into the car next to Uncle Charlie.

"Be careful," Auntie called from the warmth of the front room. And then, "Charlie, don't let those ruffians hurt the boys." I laughed to myself at her mentioning the town ruffians. That's what everybody called them—the group of teenage boys that hung around town after dark.

I'd seen them leaning against the building. They'd laugh and joke among themselves or greet the people who went by. Sometimes they'd cluster around Tucker Webb, the town cripple, and josh him in a friendly way. I thought the grown-ups misjudged them. I mean, they'd never bothered me. Sometimes they even spoke, and tongue-tied, I answered, trying to match their light-hearted tone.

As we drove along I remembered Tucker again. "Uncle Charlie, was Tucker Webb always like that?" I asked.

"Crippled, you mean?"

"Yes. The way his knees are bent, he can't even walk right. And he must stand at least a foot shorter than he would if his legs were straight."

"I guess he was born that way," Uncle replied. "He's never been able to work much, but let me tell you, he's right smart. Reads every book he gets his hands on."

We rounded a curve, and the car's headlights arched over a barren field. The wind blew dust in little circles across it. "Why'd you ask about Tucker?" Uncle said.

"Oh, I don't know. Just thought of him," I answered.

The car bounced over a particularly large hole and rolled on down the paved streets of Mesquite. Uncle Charlie drove the car to the wooden railroad station, and we all scrambled out and hurried inside. Pulling out his large pocket watch, Uncle squinted at it in the dim light of the station. "Train won't be in for at least half an hour," he declared. "Want to have a look around town?"

Of course we did. My uncle led the way, and we boys did our best to match his long stride. We passed the hardware store and post office and were headed toward the twin lights that indicated the dry goods store when we heard a commotion behind us.

"Boys, boys! What are you doing?"

"Come on, fellas. Pick him up."

"Boys. Please——"

"That's it. One, two, heave ho!"

"It's Christmas Eve, boys. You wouldn't——"

Turning around, we raced toward the voices, anxious to know what they meant. "See here," Uncle Charlie began, but no one paid the slightest attention to him.

The ruffians, the good-for-nothings. What were they doing to poor, helpless Tucker Webb?

Large youths stood on each side of the crippled man, lifting him up while he twisted in an attempt to struggle free. "Do something, Dad," Bud yelled, his eyes reflecting the surprise and fright that I felt.

But Uncle only shrugged. "Let's wait a minute. I don't think they'll hurt him."

With two carrying him and a half dozen more surrounding him, they took Tucker Webb down the street and into the dry goods store. He thrashed around and protested every inch of the way. We—and others who heard the disturbance—followed them.

Through the aisles and into the shoe section they

Tucker Webb's Christmas

went, finally setting Tucker down on a low bench in front of the rows of shoe boxes. "Clerk!" one of them called. "Come here, please. This fella needs some new shoes."

"Bet he has holes in the soles of these," another one said. "Too cold for holes in anybody's shoes."

"But I don't have any money," Tucker Webb protested. "Please, boys, let me go. Clerk! Don't measure my feet. I don't have a cent."

Bud and I watched openmouthed as the store clerk fitted shoes on him. Then another one of the hoodlums ran up with a couple pairs of heavy socks. "A man can't have new shoes and old socks," he laughed. "Here, Clerk, wrap 'em up."

The boys' chatter drowned Tucker's objections. "That man needs a new shirt. Needs two shirts. And just look at his pants. He has a patch on one knee."

A clerk wrapped up the shirts and trousers and placed them beside the shoes and socks. Then a bushy-haired youth picked up Tucker's jacket. "Just look at this," he exclaimed. "I'll bet it's five years old. How can he wear an old jacket with new pants?"

"He can't wear new shirts with an old jacket," another echoed. "That'd look awful."

"That's right, Clerk. Let's see the warmest jacket you have."

"No, no, no! Don't listen to them," Tucker cried. "I haven't got any money. I can't pay for this."

A salesman brought out several jackets and tried them on Webb despite his objections.

"Does it fit? Feel good? Do you like brown, or would you rather have blue or black?"

Tucker Webb shook his head. "It feels fine. It's beautiful. But I tell you——"

The youths stood in a cluster against the wall, smiling, laughing, poking one another. "What all do we have now, Clerk?" one asked.

"Let me see." He touched each article as he spoke. "Shoes, socks, pants, shirts, jacket. That will come to——"

"Underwear," someone called out. "It's freezing outside, and Tucker's wearing last year's long johns."

"Wrap up a pair," a short, pudgy boy ordered.

The salesman rummaged around, wrapped the underwear, and placed the package with the rest of the clothes. Taking his pad and pencil, he figured and refigured until he came up with a total.

Tucker shrugged and looked at the wooden floor. "I told you. I'm sorry, but I——"

"I'll give three dollars," a voice rang out.

"Put me down for two-fifty."

"I'll donate five."

One by one the boys came to the counter and handed the clerk some money. He counted it and glanced up. "I'm two dollars short." In a moment he had it.

Then two youths lifted Tucker to a counter. "Make a speech," they told him.

He looked from one to another, his gaze caressing the face of each of his friends. "Boys, thank you." Swallowing, he gathered pretty words from all the books he'd read. "It is with sincere thankfulness that I express my appreciation for your kind deed. What have I done to deserve such good, considerate friends? When the Lord comes, He will remind you that whatever you've done unto the least of men, you did for Him."

After a pause to nod to each of the beaming faces of the boys watching him, he continued, "My dear friends. May the God who cares for us all give you a special blessing."

Uncle Charlie studied his watch and motioned for

my cousin and me. Turning up our collars against the Texas wind, we followed him into the night.

"Uncle Charlie, did he know what they were doing?" I asked. "I mean, when they grabbed him?"

"I suspect so," he chuckled. "Fact is, they did it last year, and Tucker howled and carried on just like he did tonight."

A mile away, the train whistle split the icy air with its lonesome call. Bud, Uncle Charlie, and I huddled together, waiting. The whistle shrilled again, closer now, and we could hear the click-clacking of the engine's wheels on the steel rails. Its steam formed white clouds that seemed to freeze and hang suspended like giant cotton puffs in the star-speckled sky above it. The locomotive shrieked to a stop, and Dad was the first one we saw, his tall frame filling the vestibule doorway.

He walked down the steps, a suitcase in each hand and sacks balanced on his arms. I ran to meet him and took the heavy sacks. Chattering excitedly, we ran to the car, then drove out of the dimly lighted town into the black-felt night. Above, the stars hovered even thicker and lower and brighter. It would be a good Christmas. Perhaps the best ever.

"Grandma, I've been thinking about Uncle Bob again," Lisey sighed. *Sympathy misting her eyes, she sat on the floor in front of her grandmother's sewing table, her knees under her chin.*

"What about him, Lisey?"

"You know. His sister, Annie."

For a moment Grandma didn't answer. She held two pieces of rose cloth together and fed them under the sewing machine needle. "Almost seventy years ago when Annie died," she finally mused, *"doctors didn't* have all the know-how and medicines like we have today. In some places more families than not had a child or baby die."

"Well, I think that's crummy," Lisey exploded. She sat up straight, her chin in the air. "And nobody even cares. The world closes in and life goes on, and I think it's rotten."

"You care," Grandma answered gently. She pushed up her glasses and leaned back, thinking. "Why don't you write it down, Lisey? Go back to Uncle Bob and ask him all about it, and then write it down."

"But I don't know how to write stories. I can't even tell them well like you do."

"Maybe now you can't. But someday."

The girl stood and crossed to the window. Next door the neighbor kids romped through a sprinkler. "I like that idea." She spoke softly, slowly. "Maybe I can tell it in the junior department or somewhere."

Grandma nodded, smiling at Lisey's concern.

"And I might even write it up," Lisey told her. "And then people will know that way back before television and pocket calculators a little girl named Annie died before she had a chance to live."

"And that nearly seventy years later another young girl heard about her," Grandma added, "and cared enough to cry and to write it down."

Chapter 3

A Quilt of Comfort

"Look, Mamma. Look!" Five-year-old Bob Prestridge jumped up and down in the dusty road beside their horse-drawn wagon. "You reckon that's a car?"

His mother readjusted two-year-old Annie on her lap and peered around the wee child for a better look down the road. "Why, I do believe it is. It really is!" She continued to stare at the approaching vehicle.

"A car! I've seen a car," Bob squealed, skipping back the length of the three wagons to tell his older brothers and sisters. The dust-covered auto chugged toward the short wagon train and the eight cattle milling around it. The Prestridges gaped wide-eyed at the unfamiliar sight. His hat pushed back on his head and envy in his eyes, Father watched it pass by. Three weeks they'd been on the road. If they had owned a car, it wouldn't have taken even half that time. Only dark-eyed Annie remained unimpressed by the "speeding" vehicle. She was more interested in the pet banty rooster that had ridden on the wagon all the way from Shreveport. The little fellow flapped his wings and crowed in protest at the noisy sight. Annie laughed and clapped her hands in childish glee.

"Let's be gittin' on," Dad called. "Man says Diville's that way—straight on." He swung himself aboard the lead wagon. Mamma pulled her flowered sunbonnet down against the Texas sun and hugged Annie close as the wagon jolted over a rock. Bob and two older brothers, keeping watch on the plodding cows, ambled along beside them. Lela and Alta Mays sat primly in another wagon, too grown up to bother noticing the antics of the younger children.

Three weeks they'd been on the way from Shreveport, Louisiana, with three covered wagons their home by day and night. They traveled slowly from sunup to near sundown. The wagons could go no faster than they could herd the cattle along. Late afternoons they'd stop and make camp, and the boys would gather firewood, haul water from a nearby creek or pond, and care for the cattle.

Mamma and the girls would get out the iron Dutch oven with its long legs and set it above the campfire. By the time everybody finished the necessary chores, hot bread or biscuits would have baked inside the little square oven. Someone would rake the coals from atop its lid and, oh, how the warm bread made plain food taste so much better!

But three weeks of bumping and bouncing behind the plodding horses, of spitting out the dust that constantly hovered around them, of keeping eternal watch on the cattle, even of eating camp food as good as Mamma's, was about long enough. They'd all be glad to reach the farm near Diville, Texas, "which is near the big town of Jacksonville," as Dad had described it. The farm had a house, a barn for the animals, plenty of land to begin a garden, and acres for the children to explore. Oh, they'd all be happy to get settled.

The family arrived at Diville, a quiet farm town, the next day. Its main attraction for the children was a little boy standing up in a red toy wagon pulled by two goats. "Mamma, look!" Bob shouted, dark eyes dancing. His mother held Annie up so she too could see.

Everybody had lots of work to do to get the family moved in and the farm operating. Even before Mamma had all their possessions unpacked from the trunks and chests out of the covered wagons and had put them away to her satisfaction, Dad had the older boys with him out plowing the fields. The Prestridges planned to raise tomatoes, cotton, and corn to sell and in a year or so make enough profit to rent a larger farm from which they could bring in more money. Eventually they could buy a place of their own—at least that was their hope.

They succeeded, too. About three years later they moved to a new farm. A hundred acres, it stood near where some of their relatives lived. There the Prestridges really did work to make the farm pay. Even Bob and Annie had chores to do. The big garden always needed hoeing. Chickens had to be fed, eggs gathered, turkeys and guineas tended. And of course the cows and horses grazing in the pasture down below the house required attention.

If there wasn't enough to keep them busy with bringing in water or chasing after those silly guineas, every now and then Mrs. Prestridge would get a notion to clean the floors. Off she'd go, Bob trotting along beside her, buckets in their hands, to dig white clay. They'd spread it over the kitchen floor and the wide hallway that ran the length of the house, and then everyone would walk on it for a few days. When Mamma swept it out, the floors shone smooth and white.

Chores over each day, the children had the run of the farm—except for the peach orchard. Oh, they could play there, but the peaches belonged to old Mr. Caviness, the man from whom they rented the farm. Dire threats hung over their heads if they touched even one. Stealing! That's what it would be.

Annie and Bob were inseparable, except, of course, when cousin George came across the stream branch running between his parents' farm and the Prestridges'. Annie was a tomboy with ribbons on her dark braids, and her short legs pumped fast to keep up with Bob's longer ones.

Once Bob caught a baby sparrow hawk, and he and Annie set about to tame it. Naming it Polly, they fed it by hand and petted it until it got attached to them. They'd take Polly out to the field and set the bird down on a dead tree stump. Then Bob would grab a stick and flush a grasshopper out of the grass. Like lightning, Polly would flash down and eat it. Afterward she might fly to Annie's head, perching there until Bob stirred up another grasshopper. Finally they'd take Polly back and put her in the box on the porch. Likely as not, Mamma would have thought of something for them to do by then. Farm children worked more than they played.

The summer waned. Dusty, drooping leaves began to fall, and Mr. Prestridge counted up his profit. Pretty good, pretty good. In a couple of years they'd buy their own farm.

One day Mr. Caviness came out with a crew to pick peaches. They worked all day, and in the evening the old man knocked on Mamma's door, carrying a bushel of peaches. "I see your children's footprints all over that orchard," he told her, "but not one peach seems to be missing."

Mamma drew herself up to her full five feet. "Thank you, sir. No, they haven't touched your peaches. That would be stealing."

"Well, we'll see if we can work out some sort of arrangement next year," he smiled. "In the meantime, I hope you enjoy these."

Enjoy them they did. They ate them fresh with

cream, Mamma made pies, then she dried a few for pies later on.

Winter passed as Texas winters do, with a little snow, a lot of heavy, gray rain, a couple of ice storms, and a few weeks of damp, bone-chilling weather.

Dad started plowing at the first sign of spring, and Mamma and the children got busy planting the garden. Nothing tasted better, after long months of canned or dried foods, than those first green lettuce leaves or the crisp baby carrots. It was hard to let the new vegetables grow to full ripeness, since everyone was hungry for fresh produce.

Polly had died by then, drowned during a heavy rain. Bob and Annie had mourned her greatly, but now Annie had something else to amuse her. Dad fixed up the smokehouse into a playhouse for her. There she kept her little trinkets—broken dishes, rag dolls, and one much-prized doll with a glass face.

She would tease her brother Bob into playing in the little house with her or would tag after him instead. But George came over often, and at nine years of age, Bob felt he was becoming a bit too grown up for a mere six-year-old sister.

Late that summer Bob and George did a thoughtless thing. Never afterward could either quite remember who came up with the notion in the first place, or even why they did it. But they sneaked into the smokehouse and scattered Annie's carefully arranged toys all over the place.

The way she carried on was something else! Sobbing and crying she worked to get it back just the way she wanted it. The prank didn't seem so funny to the two boys when Annie acted so heartbroken over it. Acted like they'd murdered one of her silly rag dolls or something.

"Come help me pick peaches," Mamma called to her, offering the treat of the delicious sun-warm fruit as a balm to her feelings. Mr. Caviness had said they could have all they wanted. Mamma wouldn't strip the trees, of course, but still they picked what she termed a "right smart" number.

The family ate fresh fruit for several days, and then pies and cobblers, but Mamma had the children spread most of the peaches out on the sheds to dry.

"Sure, go ahead and eat what you want of the dried ones," she told them. "Just leave what's on the trees for Mr. Caviness, and don't eat so much you get sick."

A few days later Annie crept up beside her mother. "Mamma, my stomach hurts."

Mrs. Prestridge stopped stirring the batter and patted the little girl's head. "How does it feel?"

"I don't know. Just like—like it's sore, and it hurts."

"Even when you don't touch it?"

"Uh-huh."

"Well, let me finish stirring this cornbread, and I'll see what I can give you."

She dosed the child with some homemade medicine, a general remedy for stomach trouble. But it didn't seem to help. Annie ate only a few bites of dinner and then begged for someone to rock her. Mrs. Prestridge covered her with a patchwork quilt and held her close, rocking and crooning old camp-meeting hymns.

The little girl slept in a tiny bed in her parents' room; so it was easy for her mother to keep an eye on her. She moaned and tossed, her temperature rising. Mr. Prestridge got up and pulled her bed next to their big one so his wife could rest her hand on Annie as the girl whimpered and cried. The night seemed endless.

Morning crept in at last on a gray sky, then faintly flushing pink. The father got on the party-line telephone before the sun tipped the rim of the meadow. "Doc's coming," he said a couple of minutes later. "Couldn't tell, though, whether he was sleepy or had a hangover." He shook his head as he bent his tall frame to pat his wee daughter.

"Way he drinks, I don't know. But there's just no one else to call." Lela and Alta Mays fixed breakfast and brought a plate to Mamma. They tried to get Annie to drink some warm herb tea, but she only doubled up on her side, holding her stomach with both arms.

It seemed hours before they heard Doc Cannon's horse's hoofbeats on the rocky road leading to their house. Bob, watching from the porch, let him in the front gate. The doctor walked with just a hint of unsteadiness up the porch steps and down the wide hall to the big front bedroom.

"Bellyache, huh?" he asked gruffly. "What's she been eating?"

"Uh, I don't know." Mamma glanced up, distraught. "Nothing different from the rest of us."

"Well, let's lift her up on the big bed so I kin get a better look at her."

Mrs. Prestridge picked her up gently. The doctor pried the girl's hands off her stomach and began feeling her midsection with his large fingers. Annie screamed. Her mother clamped her hand over her own mouth. "Swollen," he muttered. "Hard and sore. Think, Mrs. Prestridge. What's she had to eat?"

Mamma rocked back and forth on the bed, stroking Annie's dark braids. "Maybe dried peaches. Yes, we've had the peaches out drying, and I saw Annie eating them a lot."

Doc Cannon grimaced. "Figured it must be something like that. Child's got locked bowels, acute constipation."

"You have medicine, don't you?" Mamma's voice held a hint of helplessness.

"Sure. Ought to help." He reached for his bag. "You have a bottle I can pour some into?"

"In the kitchen. Let me see." She hurried back with a small glass. "This'll have to do."

Cannon poured from his larger bottle into the glass. "Give her half of this now and the rest, oh, in about four hours if she still feels bad."

"Would hot and cold fomentations help?"

"Well, wouldn't hurt none. Might take down some swelling." He closed his bag. "Call me tomorrow if she's no better."

The next day she seemed worse. The doctor came again, liquor slurring his speech. He felt Annie's distended abdomen again, gave more medicine, and left.

Neighbors came and went all day, assisting with the fomentations, offering quiet advice and home remedies. The younger children stood around the door or pressed themselves against the fireplace across the room from Annie's bed. Anxious and frustrated, Mr. Prestridge came in several times during the day, worried at his inability to do anything for his daughter. Alta Mays and Lela cooked for the family and did the necessary household chores. Mamma never left Annie's side.

"You've got to sleep tonight," they told her. "We'll sit up with Annie."

She protested at first. Then, "Well, maybe I'll be better able to care for her tomorrow if I do."

By morning Annie had grown listless, lapsing into unconsciousness. In desperation they telephoned Doc Cannon again. They could hear his horse's hooves a long way off, pounding the rocky road as he galloped up. Cannon shook his head. "Done all I can. Just keep up with those fomentations."

A Quilt of Comfort

Bob, standing just inside the bedroom door, felt fear grip his heart like a cold hand deep within his chest. That Annie might actually die had been an unspoken, unacknowledged possibility. But to have the doc say so himself! The boy turned and ran outside, out to the meadow to try to find comfort in petting the horses.

Annie's breathing became more and more shallow. And she died.

Sobbing, Mamma picked her up and rocked her close against her. Kind neighbors with gentle hands and voices finally took the little girl from her mother's arms.

They brought the plain pine-wood casket into the house and set it on sawhorses in the front parlor until the funeral. The neighbors, as well as a preacher from the nearby arbor church—set up just for that summer—came to the house. Then the wagon procession made its long, dusty, slow way to the weed-grown cemetery for the funeral.

After all the fine-sounding words and prayers, and then at home, after the neighbors bearing food and comfort finally left, Bob crept slowly up the ten front steps and walked down the long hall to his room.

His mother found him there, huddled on his bed, his body shaking with more grief and sorrow than he could bear. She swallowed back her own sorrow to try to help her young son.

"We tore up her playhouse." He finally choked out the words of remorse at a harmless prank he could never reverse.

"She forgave you," Mamma murmured, stroking his black hair. "She *loved* you, Bob. You were her favorite."

"But we didn't know . . ." his voice trailed off into smothered weeping.

"Annie forgave you. She loved you," Mamma repeated. "Her love and the happy times you two had——no one can take them away."

With tears still spilling down his cheeks, Bob raised his head. "Did you——" He choked, then began again, "Did you know that, that her footprints are still . . . in the garden and under the trees?"

"I know," she sighed, grief lodging in her throat. "I know." She stroked his hair, rubbed his shoulders. "Do you remember what the preacher read this afternoon?" she asked after a time.

"No."

"He was reading from the Bible—from 1 Thessalonians 4:13 and 16 through 18. Paul is—well, this is what he says: 'I would not have you to be ignorant, brethren, concerning them which are asleep,' " she began slowly, quietly, her voice familiar, with the old-new words of hope, " 'that ye sorrow not, even as others which have no hope. . . .

" 'For the Lord himself shall descend from heaven with a shout, with the voice of the archangel, and with the trump of God: and the dead in Christ shall rise first: then we which are alive and remain shall be caught up together with them in the clouds, to meet the Lord in the air: and so shall we ever be with the Lord.' "

Pausing, she caressed her son. "And Paul, writing this, knew how we would feel, and he added, 'Wherefore comfort one another with these words.'

"You'll see Annie again, Bob. And God—well, He doesn't cause these things. Sin—that's what does it. God loves us, and He suffers and grieves with us." She blinked back the tears threatening to destroy her composure. "And God has given us this hope, this comfort of knowing we'll live forever with Him—and Annie."

She hugged her son, and love flowed through her arms, somehow making him feel better. "Go to sleep now, Bob. We'll talk again in the morning."

He nodded, and she tiptoed from his room. So, hugging close the memory of his mother's words—God's words spoken through Paul—around him like one of her warm, worn patchwork quilts, he fell asleep.

"Hey, Grandma, lookee here. Guess what I got!" Lisey let the door slam behind her and raced through the house till she found her grandmother in the kitchen fixing supper.

"Mrs. Maloney gave me ten dollars. Can you believe it?" She waved the crisp bill in the air, doing a double-step jig.

Grandma was duly impressed. "For one afternoon's work?" she puzzled. "Lisey, are you sure you're worth it?"

"She said it was worth it to her to get her kitchen waxed and the windows cleaned." The girl sank against a kitchen stool. "Let me tell you, I worked. But ten dollars! Do you know what this makes?"

"How much?"

"One hundred even."

"That's wonderful, Lisey. And the summer isn't even half over." She dropped chopped onions into sizzling margarine and stirred with an expert hand. "Between cleaning and baby-sitting you'll have half your tuition before the summer's gone."

"Well—maybe. But that's not bad for an inexperienced kid, huh?"

"I've been thinking about you all day," Grandma told her. "Have you heard Mr. Smith tell his stories?"

"Mr. Smith at church?"

"The same."

"I didn't know he had any stories."

"Oh, yes. He's been telling them to the juniors every

now and then, and I just recently realized that he began work at fourteen, too."

"What did he do?"

"Colporteuring."

"You've got to be kidding. I'd be scared to pieces."

"He was one gutsy kid, let me tell you." She added raw potatoes and hot water, then put a lid on the soup. "Anyway, he's been putting his experiences on tapes and—"

"I'd love to hear them," Lisey interrupted.

"And I'm a step ahead of you," her grandmother grinned. "That's why I asked him if we could borrow the tapes. Thought we could listen to them as I help you with your crocheting sometimes."

"I'm not doing anything tonight."

Grandma laughed. "Tonight, then."

Lisey stretched, then crossed the kitchen. "I'll make the hoecakes," she volunteered, opening a cabinet door. "You know, Grandma, I've gotten real interested in old-timey stories ever since Daddy and Uncle Bob told me about Tucker Webb and Annie. I just never knew that people had such interesting lives, even without cars and TV. Guess I kinda thought most people just sat around and did nothing."

"You're talking about my era too," Grandma laughed. "In fact, if you're serious about collecting old-time stories, you ought to get your mother to tell you about Mary Moore."

"Who's she?"

"Your mother knew her a few years back." She lifted the lid and stirred the soup before she turned the fire down to simmer. "That little lady had done more before she was thirty than many people do in a lifetime." She stepped across the kitchen for some flour and water. "Here, Lisey, I'll make the 'rivvels' while you do the

A Quilt of Comfort

hoecakes. We'll get supper ready quickly that way."

"But what about Mary Moore?" Lisey poured boiling water over yellow cornmeal and stirred it. She pucked her mouth up as she always did when she was disappointed.

"Let's stick to Mr. Smith's adventures for now," Grandma said. "Miss Moore—she's a whole different story."

Chapter 4

The Silent Customer

I was fourteen years old and wanted to be a colporteur. That's what they called literature evangelists back then. Brother Harrison's talk did it—the tremendous experience he told! All the excitement—and money for school too. By the time I left that Sabbath afternoon meeting, I knew I couldn't be happy spending the summer any other way. So I signed up.

But as I said, I was only fourteen, just out of the eighth grade and still in knee britches. Yet, I'd be fifteen by summer, and that gave me a spot of courage. Besides, as Brother Harrison had told me, Jesus was only twelve when He began His work.

Naturally I felt timid about approaching my folks on the subject, and I was afraid the other kids would tease me. There were six of us in the family, and I just couldn't bring it up in front of everyone. So, writing a note to my mother, I stuck it between two dinner plates in the cupboard where she'd be sure to find it after supper. Then I tiptoed around all weak-kneed, my heart in my throat, until finally everyone else was in bed and Mother called me.

"I have talked it over with your father," she began in her gentle voice, "and if you like our plan, you may go."

I could do it! I'd be a colporteur, having fun and actually earning money for school tuition. My thoughts soared away on the wings of Brother Harrison's adventures. As Mother continued I could hardly coax my mind back to listen.

"I've talked to your sister Pearl, and since she wants to sell books too, we think you two might work up in Bowie, Texas. That way you'll be near your aunt, and she can keep an eye on you. I'd feel easier if you kids were near each other. Maybe Pearl can stay with Aunt Nellie."

I nodded happily. "Anything you say, Mom."

But I'd still be on my own, I thought, earning money and doing something worthwhile too—almost like a real preacher, having the chance to share my knowledge of Christ with people all day long.

So it was settled. We went to Bowie, about sixty miles from our home in Keene. Pearl would take the city, while I would sell in the country. Despite the hard work and long hours I knew awaited me, I was excited. Luckily I had no idea how many miles I'd walk before the summer ended.

J. O. Wilson, the field secretary, went along to help us get under way. As we went through Fort Worth, Elder Wilson stopped just long enough for me to get a haircut. I guess I could have let it offend me when he suggested it, but I didn't. Just anxious to get going.

I had a new pair of shoes that fit pretty tight, but I figured they'd stretch after I walked a bit. They did—but oh, those first few days! I never knew a mile could be so long.

The town contained enough homes to keep Pearl busy all summer. I'd take everything outside the city limits: the homes, ranches, and farms dotting the gently rolling countryside around Bowie. Sorry-looking land it was, actually. Full of rocks, ditches, and eroded-out ravines, but it raised corn and cotton and a lot of cattle.

I sold "cold turkey"—that is, without the leads most

The Silent Customer

of the literature evangelists have now. Never missed a house. That was one thing they drilled into us, never—but *never*—skip a house.

At night it would have been too far to go back to Aunt Nellie's; so I'd always ask the people if I could spend the night with them. No one ever refused me. I'd help with the chores—nothing new to me—eat supper, and sack out in a spare bedroom, or in a room with one of the boys, maybe even on the floor.

Baths were somewhat of a problem. After walking all day long under the Texas sun, I got powerfully dusty and sweaty. People around there bathed in tin washtubs in the kitchen or backyard, so naturally no one thought to offer me a bath. When I started out from my aunt's every Monday morning, I carried four extra white shirts in my little case, and I quickly learned to take advantage of any isolated stream or pond I came across for bathing. Don't get me wrong, that was no hardship—only exciting and fun.

One evening toward the end of the summer I came upon a farmhouse, and noticing a man, Mr. Phillips was his name, milking out in the barn, I stepped up to him and asked if he had an extra stool. I began milking alongside him, and I wasn't any greenhorn about it, either. I'd milked cows morning and night for as long as I could remember. I also introduced myself, told him what I was doing, and asked if I might spend the night.

"Be glad to have you, glad to have you," Mr. Phillips assured me. "We have one boy, but he's gone for the evening to a birthday party. Won't be home till pretty late. And he gets up before dawn to begin plowing, so I don't reckon you'll see him. Anyhow, glad to have you." We finished the milking, he put aside the stools, and we picked up our full, foaming buckets. "Come on in," he called over his shoulder.

I followed him into the house, and he introduced me to his wife. I had just enough time to show him my book, *Our Day in the Light of Prophecy*, before Mrs. Phillips called us to dinner. And what a dinner! After walking up and down those hills all day, I was famished, and you'd better believe I ate. They had pie on the table, but I passed it by, expecting to have it for dessert. Then realizing they were eating it first, I took some. Although I'd never seen anything like it before, it was delicious. An Irish potato pie, rather like a cobbler, and it was great. Plenty of milk, vegetables, and homemade light bread too. I could hardly stop eating long enough to carry on a polite conversation.

"Where do you get this worshiping on Saturday for Sunday?" Mr. Phillips asked, not unkindly but simply interested. "I think you must do it because of tradition."

I swallowed a mouthful of that good potato pie, took a long drink of cold milk, and sat quietly to see what he was leading up to. "After supper let's go into the living room," he continued, "and I'll show you from the Bible where you're wrong. I fear you're a Seventh-day Adventist just because your mamma and papa were. Don't blame you, you understand," he added gently, "and I don't say you're misled on purpose, just confused about what the Bible says."

Nodding, I smiled. "I'll be glad to talk with you about it," I told him. "I always enjoy talking about the Bible and like to listen to other viewpoints. If I'm wrong, I want to know it."

Dinner over, we went into the living room and made small talk till Mrs. Phillips finished her after-dinner cleaning of the kitchen. When she joined us, we all sat down in the neat little room, and I waited for Mr. Phillips to speak.

"Now, just where in the Bible do you get this wor-

The Silent Customer

shiping on Saturday?" he began.

Sending a quick prayer to God for the Holy Spirit to guide my words, I opened my case and took out my book and my Bible. Turning to the chapter in the subscription book on the Sabbath, I scanned it, then opened the Bible. Beginning with Genesis 2, I explained that God made the Sabbath to memorialize His creation of the world and that it was holy whether anyone observed it or not. Then I turned to Exodus 20 and read the fourth commandment.

I showed them from the Bible that Christ and His followers kept the Sabbath. Then, reading from *Our Day in the Light of Prophecy,* I explained how, after Christ's death, Sunday observance crept into the early church.

Mr. and Mrs. Phillips didn't say a word. Naturally I hoped I wasn't being obnoxious or superior-sounding. The last thing in the world I wanted to do was offend them. Watching their silent, solemn faces, I had no idea what was going on in their minds. I went all the way through the chapter, and when I finally finished, the man didn't say a thing, not a thing to try to disprove me. We talked on general subjects for a few minutes, then he noted it was getting late. "Our boy sleeps on a cot under the trees in the front yard," he said. "We keep an extra cot out there just for people who come passing through and need a bed; so you're welcome to it."

Tired—bone-tired—I assured them that a cot would be fine. And it was. The night was comfortably warm. I guess I fell sound asleep before I had time to turn over. Sometime later the piercing screech of a peafowl in a nearby tree seemed to split the night wide open. It practically scared me out of my skin. I lay dead-still in the darkness, and my heart pounded triple time until I realized what it was. Pulling the cover over my head, I went back to sleep.

I guess I overslept, because the sun was climbing when I opened my eyes. Across the fields I could see a young boy plowing. When I went to the house to thank the Phillipses for my bed, Mr. Phillips surprised me by asking if he could buy a book, "Right now, if possible." Because it was nearly the end of the summer and I wouldn't have time to place orders and get the books back before school started, I carried a few extra in my bag and sold him a copy before I left.

As I walked down the dusty road, past the sun-seared corn and cotton, an uneasiness about the Bible study I'd given them weighed on my mind. I wondered if I'd come on too strong, wondered if I'd been a good representative of the church, wondered what they'd do if they ever met another Seventh-day Adventist, wondered . . .

Time passed. I went back to academy, then college, spent several years in California, came back to Houston, and finally returned home. Occasionally I'd think of the Phillipses, curious if they'd read the book. You know how you wonder if anything ever came of something you did. The Holy Spirit prompts someone to buy a book. But then what? Somehow that particular family stood out in my mind more than any other contacts I'd made, and I half wished I could stop by and see them sometime. Couldn't think of a nonawkward way to do it, though.

Then one time when I visited the Fort Worth church, my Sabbath School class teacher had some extra time and began telling how he came into the church. "A young boy came by my folks' house just outside of Bowie, Texas, in late August. He was selling *Our Day in the Light of Prophecy*," he said.

My ears perked up, and I leaned forward to hear better.

"I was away that evening," he went on, "but my dad

asked the boy why he kept Saturday, and the young man sat down and talked at least an hour. He read text after text, and by the time he finished, my folks were speechless. They bought the book, read it, and immediately accepted Seventh-day Adventism. They sent me to school at Keene that same year. I finished there, went on to become a teacher, and—well, here I am now."

Chapter 5

The Recluse

I'd barely begun selling books that first summer, just got my speech down where I didn't stutter all over the sales talk as I gave it, and they sprang Big Week on me. In case you've never encountered the term, Big Week is one special week when all the literature evangelists in a given area engage in a sort of friendly competition. Everyone tries to outsell the others during Big Week, and I was a little shook up about it.

It was bad enough having the nickname Baby Colporteur tagged onto me, and I knew that if I didn't try with every ounce of effort I possessed, I'd be at the bottom when it came to sales. After all, what could I expect, out on the road for the first time in my life and the youngest colporteur in Texas at that. Somehow I just had to be a little way up on the list of big sellers.

The first thing, I decided, was to find some good territory with the houses close together. Around Bowie it was mostly farmland or ranches, and I'd waste hours tramping past acres of corn and cattle country as I went from home to home. So I climbed to the top of a big hill they called Rock Mountain, where I could see practically the whole county spread out like a patchwork quilt below. And down to my right I noticed a thickly populated area a few miles away where the houses clustered fairly close together.

Saying a prayer, I scrambled down Rock Mountain and started out. At the first house a Baptist minister met me at the door. I showed him my book, *Our Day in the Light of Prophecy.* He asked what church I represented, and I told him Seventh-day Adventist.

"Well, you're wrong," he declared, "but you have a good book there. I think I'll take it."

"Wow! If only all of my sales would be that easy," I thought, "I might make the middle of the Big Week list."

Farther down the road I came to a wire gate and could see a faint road snaking through the high field grass. Beyond the field, just barely perceptible in a grove of trees, hid the peak of an old house. *Pass it by* was my first impulse. After all, it was Big Week. Why waste time—precious time—hunting down an old house that might not even have anybody living in it? But Brother Harrison's words clouted me over the head and turned me toward the gate. "Don't miss a house, don't miss a house, *don't miss a house!*"

"OK," I thought, "I won't miss it. I'll come back and get it after Big Week." Leaving the gate, I started to walk on down the road.

"Don't miss a house," he'd said. "You just never know whom you might be passing by. Never again might you have a chance to meet that person. Don't miss a house."

Kicking a clod with my already scuffed-up new shoes, I retraced my steps. At least I could see if I could open the gate. Impossible. Someone had wound so much wire tightly around it and the post that I could have worked all day and never gotten it open without a tool of some kind. However, with a little investigation, I realized that I could spread the fence wires apart and crawl through that way.

But I didn't want to. The sun already shone hot and

bright above me. Once again I started down the dusty road. "Don't miss a house." How ridiculous, how dumb, to go to so much effort. "You never know whom you're passing by." Once more I turned back and crawled between the wires.

With weeds clinging to my socks, I tramped through the field and on through a bit of timber until finally I came to the house. A fence at least seven feet high surrounded it, with barbed wires not more than six inches apart stretched tight between the posts. Many people had fences around their homes because wolves still roamed the area. Whoever lived here must have really been afraid of them. There seemed no way through the fence. I couldn't see any gate. But since I'd come this far, it would be a waste of time to give up now.

So I found a stick and propped the wire open. I was skinny—real skinny—and it wasn't too hard to crawl between the strands. After I'd walked a few feet toward the house, a huge dog hurtled off the porch and rushed straight at me. He tore at the ground, and his mouth snapped open and shut with incredible speed as he growled and barked. I froze, simply paralyzed.

"Git him! Git him!" a man shouted from the porch.

"That dog could rip off my head with one bite," I thought wildly. I'd never seen such huge jaws, such a mammoth dog before. I couldn't run. It would have been futile anyway with the seven-foot fence.

"Git him!" his master commanded, and in that instant I glanced past the dog plunging at my neck. A man—the biggest one I'd ever seen—stood on the porch, his face contorted with anger, his hand fingering a gun on his hip.

"Lord, here I am," I breathed.

The dog hurled himself at my neck, stopped short, put an immense paw on each of my shoulders, almost pushing me down with his weight, and—licked my face. It was as if he'd recognized me as a friend.

At the same instant the air turned blue with the man's expletives. "You're trespassing!" he shouted. "Why do you think I have a fence here, anyway?"

The dog got down, pacing along beside me, his tail wagging ninety miles an hour.

"Now git out. Git out the same way you came in."

Believe me, I turned and ran as he punctuated his words with a few shots into the ground by my feet. I crawled through the fence as the dog slobbered his good-bye to me, and I scooted away from that gun faster than I'd dreamed I could go.

It seemed a long way through the timber and through the pasture to the gate I'd crawled through twenty minutes before. I put myself back together as best I could and started down the road again. " 'Don't miss a house,' Brother Harrison had said, huh? Well, I'd sure have a good story to tell him."

The rest of the day I did well, however. I didn't pass by a house. And I made a sale at every stop. A dozen times I thanked God for saving my life back there and for helping me sell so many books that it made up for the time I'd wasted—until late afternoon.

I'm ashamed to admit it, and I didn't even want to recognize the fact myself, but I got lost. The roads winding and crisscrossing through the timberland confused me, and I had trouble recalling the homes I'd visited and those I hadn't. Looking down from the hill early that morning, the twisting roads hadn't seemed so perplexing. Walking on them, step by step by step, past acres of trees and look-alike white frame houses, I couldn't tell head or tail about where I was.

After I'd walked along a narrow road through the trees for several minutes without seeing any houses, I spotted the peak of a house surrounded by timber just ahead. I was awfully glad to see it. At least someone could point me the way out of the woods, so I headed straight for it.

And to this day I can't imagine why I didn't recognize where I was. Coming up from the opposite direction, I guess the house simply looked different. You'd think that propping up the fence wires so I could crawl through would have made some impression, though. But then, I'd crawled through other fences that day because, as I said, people had them to keep out the wolves.

The dog gave me the first clue. Here he came, bounding off the porch, tail wagging to beat the band, his tongue lolling out of that huge mouth which almost seemed to be smiling at me—he was that glad to see me. I braced myself as he jumped up to my shoulders and licked my face.

I petted the monstrous beast, forgetting for a moment that I'd have his master to contend with. Then the man came, brandishing his gun in the air. "I told you if I ever saw you near here again, I'd shoot you on sight!" he shouted, running toward me.

My heart plummeted. Turning, I stumbled and fell, and my book dropped out of my hands, flipping over and landing faceup. It lay open with pictures of the beasts of Daniel 7 toward the man. He strode up, stopping at my feet. "Whatta you trying to do," he snarled, "scare me with those pictures?"

And I looked up, up, up, past his dirty boots that rose taller than my waist (if I'd been standing) till my eyes reached his face. "No, sir," I stammered. "That's from the Bible."

When he didn't move farther—just looked at me—I picked up the book and began to give him my sales talk. Laying down his gun in the dust, he watched me with a curious expression as I went from chapter to chapter—flipping the pages, showing him the pictures, and explaining what the book taught. Upon finishing, I waited, unsure as to what I should do next. Then he spoke. "Do you think there's hope for someone like me?"

His quiet question exploded in my mind like the gunshots from his weapon had earlier that day. "Why, yes——" I began.

"Now wait before you answer," he commanded. "You don't know what kind of a man I am. I've robbed. I've even murdered. Why, boy, there's nothing I haven't done. Could God possibly save a person like *me*?"

"God can save you the same as anyone else," I told him. "The same as the best person you can think of. We aren't saved because we're good. Rather, we're saved because we recognize that we're sinners and because we accept Christ's blood to make up for our sinfulness. Besides," I added, "you know the story of Paul on the way to Damascus. He'd even murdered Christians just because they worshiped Christ. But Christ stopped him on the road to Damascus. He accepted Christ right there, and in that instant his life changed. All you need to do now is accept Christ's grace to cover your sins."

"Well, I'm sorry I did you that way," he said. "You might be the best friend I've ever met. Will you not tell anybody about my living here?" he asked, a strange pleading note tingeing his words. "I'm hiding out here. Don't never leave except at night sometimes."

"Of course, I won't tell anyone," I assured him, "only I just wish you'd read the book and accept Christ. You'll have a different life if you do."

He scratched his scraggly beard with a rough hand. "I reckon I'd buy one of your books if you didn't have to come back to bring it to me. I watch this place very carefully, and I wouldn't want the dog to hurt you or maybe me to take a shot at you because I didn't realize who you are."

Picking up my case from the ground, I replied, "I keep an extra book with me just for people who won't be around at the end of the summer for delivery. I'd be glad to let you have it."

So I took his money, gave him the book, and he helped me through the fence. "If you ever do come out here again," he called as I made my way through the timber, "you might whistle or something as you come up so I'll know you."

"Thank you," I shouted back, "and may God bless you."

Incidentally, I had the largest sales record of any of the Texas colporteurs that week—my first Big Week.

Chapter 6

Thunderstorm

Out in the inky night the rain fell in torrents as if trying to drown the earth. Huddled under the tarpaulin in a leaky brush-arbor church, I shivered more from fear of the storm than from the chill. Then they attacked—the mosquitoes. They covered my face, neck, and bare arms, and I couldn't hit at them fast enough even to slow down their chewing on my raw skin.

Colporteuring! This was colporteuring? This the ideal way to spend the summer? And how had I gotten myself into this immediate predicament—escaping nearly drowning in a Texas thunderstorm only to be eaten alive by giant mosquitoes?

It was my own fault, of course. I'd been working in a timber area—couldn't see which way the road went because of the trees—and had gotten lost. Under normal conditions I could always find a house and request someone to point me toward town. But I hadn't had the foresight to ask to bed down at the last place I visited. Suddenly I found myself at dusk with an incredibly black cloud hovering lower and lower above me, and no houses were in sight.

Then the rain. Not the gentle pitter-patter of a spring shower. No way! All at once the bottom fell out of the sky. Somehow God was looking out for me—but not in the way I thought. There in the pasture near where I stood in a sodden daze rose a brush-arbor church.

Now I guess a lot of people have never heard of such a thing, but I'll describe it briefly. To make a meeting place, the people would put poles into the ground to form a base, and then they would make a roof with brush. It provided shade but virtually no protection from such a downpour as was drenching me. This particular arbor church contained benches, and it seated about two hundred.

As lightning slashed across the sky, I spotted a piano covered with a tarpaulin. I ran to it, crawled under the tarp, and sat there, waiting for the rain to stop.

The whole countryside rumbled with thunder. The ground seemed to vibrate beneath me as the claps rolled across the sky. Drawing my knees up under my chin, I closed my eyes against the smothering darkness and waited for the storm to pass.

Then the mosquitoes struck. Dozens of them, all biting at once. I slapped at them, but it was a losing battle. Two choices, I decided: stay under the tarp and get eaten alive or go out and get myself drowned. I opted for the drowning, leaving my bag with its book, order pad, and extra clothes under the tarp.

Creeping out into the arbor, I ducked my head as the rain cascaded through the brush. Another crack of lightning ripped through the black clouds, and I could see an old-fashioned coal-oil lantern hanging nearby. As soon as the lightning speared the sky again, I got the lantern and dipped my handkerchief into the oil. Then I crawled back under the tarp to bathe my face and hands with the fluid in the hope of discouraging the buzzing, stinging pests.

But before I could raise the cloth to my face, a wind blew under the tarp, lifting it up and taking all the mosquitoes with it. It took a moment for me to realize

Thunderstorm

what had happened. All I could say was, "Thank You, Lord. I really appreciate that."

The thunder roared, trying to tear the sky apart. I could hear the rain pounding the tarp above me and could see the lightning's flash even through my heavy shelter. "This is ridiculous," I reasoned. "I'll be here all night. When and if the rain stops, I've no place to go. Might as well try to get me some sleep."

Putting my bag under my head, I stretched out beside the piano. Beneath me the platform vibrated from the rain and thunder. Darkness pressed in so thick I could taste it—a bitter taste filling my mouth, choking me.

I was scared, if you want to know the truth. And you can shake your head at the mentality of a fifteen-year-old who sings himself to sleep, but I remembered the song "Anywhere With Jesus." My voice wouldn't have won any prizes, but at least it kept me company, and the words brought peace. I dozed off.

I've no idea how long I slept, but the next thing I knew, a heavy hand on my shoulder was shaking me awake. A flashlight blinded my eyes. I squinted up at two policemen above me. "What are you doing?" the one who held me demanded.

"I'm sleeping," I answered. Not too witty an answer, I have to admit.

"You know what I mean. Who are you? a runaway? Where do you live?"

Sitting up, I eased away from his grip. "I sell books," I said, reaching behind me to get my bag. I pulled out *Our Day in the Light of Prophecy*. Starting in with the Bible as a whole, I explained how Christ was its center, and how the history and fulfillment of prophecy testified to its inspiration. Chapter by chapter I gave my sales talk outlining the book. Signs of the Second Coming, the activity of the little horn, the origin of evil, on down to Armageddon, the millennium, and the new earth.

When I finally finished, we all three just stood there a moment, and I realized the rain had stopped. "I got caught in the storm," I added. "Guess I went to sleep."

The first policeman took the book from my hands. Cradling the flashlight in one elbow, he leafed through it and came to the final blank pages where I'd written the names of those who'd given me orders. "Why, I know him," the officer exclaimed, pointing to the lead name. "And there's Mrs. Silvester and Miss Marylou Cassey. Mr. Dateweather! You mean you sold that old rascal one of these books? Good for you."

He reached into his pocket and took out his pencil. I watched in amazement as he added his own name and address to the list. "Now you go on back to sleep," he told me. "This brush arbor's on our nightly checklist. We'll be by a couple more times to be sure you're OK."

They left—their boots squishing in the soggy earth and their flashlights making pale, bobbing circles in the night. I lay down on the platform, my bag under my head, eyes open toward the black sky. But somehow the night didn't seem dark anymore.

Chapter 7

The Lounger

During my second summer the conference publishing secretary sent me to work in Greenville, Texas, a small town fifty miles northeast of Dallas. I'd take the farmland surrounding the town, and my sister and her girl friend would sell in the city itself. I was lucky—or more accurately, blessed—to find a family who would take me in for the summer. They even had a son my age. Spending weekends on their farm—which gave me sort of a home base—I'd help with the chores.

I arrived in Greenville in early summer while the trees and grass still held a dewy, new-green look and the cotton plants and corn grew like small emeralds against the velvet black fields. Getting off at the train station, I noticed three young men lounging against a baggage cart and decided to practice my sales talk on them. If I couldn't get through it without stumbling around, I figured I'd better go off and give it to the trees again. To my delight one of them said he wanted the volume.

"I'll take your order now," I told him, "but I can't deliver it till the end of summer. You can pay then."

One of the others said he'd be interested, but he lived out of town. The third, a giant of a youth, only asked when I made my deliveries. "About the first of September," I replied. "Maybe a bit earlier. I have to be back in school soon after that."

"You mean you deliver all the books you've sold all summer?" he questioned further. "You mean you don't collect your money till then?"

"Maybe he's trying to figure out if he can save the money for one," I thought, and I explained the system of order and delivery to him again. But he wouldn't commit himself.

"Maybe later," he evaded. "I'll see you around."

And that he did. Every week when I came into town to get my mail, it just happened that I had to walk across the railroad yards. Various steam engines stood near the station, the smell of coal smoke filled the air, and that same young man always leaned against a baggage cart. Always he'd stop me, always act interested in the book, but wouldn't say whether he would buy a copy or not. "No, not today," he'd say. "Maybe later." And without fail, he questioned me about my deliveries.

Maybe I should have been suspicious of him, but I just didn't pay him that much attention. I did wonder what he—such a great hulk of humanity—did for a living. Once I asked him if he worked around the railroad station. "Naw, I'm just killin' time," he muttered.

"Well, where do you work?"

"Nowhere nowadays. Don't have a job."

Maybe that's why he can't order a book, I reasoned in my naiveté.

The weeks passed, one hot day after another. Flies buzzed me as I hiked up and down the country roads, past fields of waist-high corn, then shoulder-high corn. Past acres of tall, dusty cotton, each plant covered with full, fat, fluffy bolls. Late August arrived before I was ready for it. The time had come to make plans to return to school, to wind up all the loose ends of the summer, and to think about deliveries.

It was on Friday that I made the mistake. I knew

The Lounger

better, but Sabbath was coming on; so I kept right on making deliveries as long as I could before sundown. By the time I reached the last home and circled back into town, the bank had closed, and I was left with my overstuffed money bag. I'd have to walk the couple of miles into the country to my weekend home—just me and my money on those deserted roads.

Normally I wouldn't have given it a second thought. Country people were friendly, accommodating. If someone came by, I was sure to get a ride. But nibbling away at the back of my mind was the thought of that young man in town. That overly friendly, overly interested-in-me-and-my-deliveries, great big hulk of a guy. An uneasiness surrounded me, darker than the graying sky.

"Surely he won't be lying in wait for me out on the road," I told myself, adding a firm command to stop dramatizing the situation. Besides, God was with me. I was doing His task, and He'd helped me a hundred times already, what with orders and a different bed every night. No need to get jumpy this late in the summer.

I straightened my shoulders and tried not to look as tired as I felt. I came to the depot, peeked around the corner, and breathed an audible sigh of relief. My unwanted friend was nowhere in sight. Gaining confidence, I strode on about six steps, then——

"Hi, there. How are you doin'?" My knees turned to jelly as a too familiar big arm grabbed me around my neck. "You delivering your books now, huh?"

"Not at the moment," I stammered past my frozen larynx. "Too late."

"But you have been," he persisted, half matching my steps and half dragging me along.

"Well—yes, I have been."

We walked about two blocks, past the streetlights, past the well-lighted homes of Greenville, toward a dark stretch where I knew we'd see no one and no one'd see us. "He'll get me there," I thought, trying with every ounce of my brain to figure a way of escape. There was no way, I tell you. No way.

Did I mention that he was big? And did I tell you that I was kind of small for my sixteen years? He had me around my wrist, his fingers lapping around it. Every time we'd go under a streetlight I could see that my hand was turning blue from lack of circulation. It felt numb, and I couldn't move my fingers. He wasn't about to let me get away.

Already he'd slapped me on my hip pocket and felt that full bag of money. Let me tell you, I was scared. "Lord, I'm in Your hands," I told God as we entered the dark area. "I'm helpless."

And God performed a miracle right there.

There were no crossroads in the unlighted section of street and no reason for a traffic jam, but, of all things—cars were in a bottleneck stalled crossways in the street, their lights shining in all directions. It was practically like broad daylight. He didn't have a chance to do a thing. We marched through there, his hand around my wrist, and came to a residential stretch again.

I began to have some hope. "Thank You, Lord," I prayed. Surely there would be some way of escape, since God had protected me back there. So I thought I'd try conversation, try to get his hand off my nearly paralyzed wrist. "Where are you going out here this late at night?" I asked in what I hoped was a normal voice.

I felt rather than heard the sneering laughter on his face. "Just goin' to see a man about a dog."

We trotted on. On past streetlights, past friendly porch lights, past open windows with people inside reading as they relaxed on the warm summer night. Town ended in a few more houses, and beyond that lay the blackest fields and the blackest night you can imagine. I knew if he got me out there, I wouldn't have a chance—not a chance.

Would he break my arm and grab the money? I wondered. Or knock me down and beat me up? Whatever, with each step I felt that I was walking that much nearer to my fate. Every step, every breath, was a prayer.

Just as we got to the last house I realized I knew the man sitting inside. With no effort at all—and I mean no effort—I slipped my wrist out of his iron grasp and ran up to the porch. "This is where I stop," I called back as I hammered on the big French doors. At least the man would let me in the house. Beyond that, I had no plan.

There was no reply.

Becoming desperate, I knocked louder. I peeked through the curtain, and there, hidden behind his newspaper and just a few feet in front of me, he sat, idly turning the pages, oblivious to my situation. "Mr. Calverston! Mr. Calverston!" I shouted, terror tingeing my voice. "It's me. Hugh." The man made no answer, no hint that he knew I was there.

I couldn't stay on the porch forever. That big guy could come back and drag me off. So I ran off the front porch and around to a side porch hidden in the darkness from the street.

"Did God bring me this far just to let me get out of my mess the best way I could?" I thought wildly. Then, jumping off the porch, I crawled under a big workbench, hoisting myself up under the 1 by 12s on each side. I lay there, able to see down and out in front of me. And there, just inches from my eyes, stood the feet of my attacker. Hidden in shadows, he watched the man inside the house.

Hardly daring to breathe, I clung to the boards, my heartbeat echoing in every pulse and seeming to boom out in the stillness. Suddenly my nose tickled, and I realized I'd sniffed up some of the pine dust from the bench. Any second I'd sneeze.

"He'll kill me," I thought. "He'll hear me, and he'll be so mad he'll drag me out and kill me." Somehow I moved with the speed of a snail and managed to press my nose against my knuckle as I grasped the board. The urge to sneeze faded.

Minutes crept by, measured by the loud thud-thud of my heart. My arms ached, my back hurt, my throat was so dry I thought I'd choke. Just when I thought I couldn't hang under the bench any longer, the boy slowly walked away.

I watched him go past the squares of window light, down the sidewalk, under the first streetlight, on down the street, then clear out of sight. Carefully I eased myself from under the bench and started in the opposite direction. Out in the darkness, vocalizing softly to no one but myself and the stars—and God—I sang, "God will take care of you," and so full of thankfulness was I that I wouldn't have cared who heard me.

Chapter 8

The Secret

I walked down the steps, a battered suitcase in each hand and with the taste of loneliness dry in my mouth. I'd pulled it off real well, I thought, taking the first step on the dusty road between Bowie and Decatur. My aunt, all tearful and worried, hovered around as I put my clean clothes in one case and my colporteur books in another.

"I'd feel so much better if you knew where you're going to live once you get there," she sighed.

And I'd answered with a careless confidence I didn't feel: "Oh, God has always found a bed for me as I worked around here. I guess He'll do it again."

The sun, already busy drying the dew on the cotton fields, felt good through the cool morning air. "Might as well enjoy it before it gets up a little higher and begins to roast me," I thought.

I'd had a good summer in Bowie, selling *Our Day in the Light of Prophecy*, and I'd discovered that when I asked God to be with me every step of the way, I was successful. But I'd finished that territory before time to return to school, so they had sent me to Decatur.

And there lay my problem—no place to stay when I got there. I'd used my aunt's place as a home base in Bowie, somewhere to come back to on weekends. I didn't have enough money to stay in a hotel or "Y" even if the town had them. I hoped there was at least a boardinghouse where I could light for the night. Maybe it wouldn't cost too much. You see, I had no cash coming in except an occasional quarter from the small books I carried with me. I used this cash for different essentials, and since the beginning of summer, I'd learned that some essentials weren't.

Late afternoon when I made it to Decatur, my feet were tired—as they were after walking miles every day—and my arms ached from the unaccustomed weight of my luggage. After checking my bags in the train depot, I took a long cool drink of water, then headed into town.

Now apprehension threatened to engulf the excitement of going to a new town, and I began to talk to God as I walked along.

"All right, God," I told Him, in the easy one-friend-to-another way of praying I'd discovered that summer. "This is where You come in. I know You've promised to help me, and now's the time. I'll appreciate it."

I turned onto the main street and passed a general store, a yard-goods store, a little grocery store. "You know that I need a place to sleep tonight, and if You send me back to the depot to lean on a bench, that's OK. But it would surely be nice if You could send me to someone special, someone that's open to learning about You."

Deciding to walk all around the square before going out on the side streets, I turned the corner. A few old men sat whittling in front of the courthouse. Others pitched horseshoes in the sun-bleached Bermuda grass. Sparrows twittered in the gnarled mesquite trees. The sun made long shadows across the lawn.

"Why, don't I know you?"

I spun toward the excited voice behind me. There stood a woman—early forties, I'd guess—and I'd never seen her before in my life. "No, ma'am. I don't believe you do," I said, feeling awkward and embarrassed.

She looked at me so intently that I could feel my ears turning red, even though she had kind gray eyes under her knitted brows. Slowly she shook her head. "Is your name Smith? Tom Smith?"

Now my mouth did fall open. "No, ma'am, but that's my dad's name."

"Oh, my dear, now I am embarrassed," she fluttered. "Of course, you couldn't be Tom. He's my age, but——" She broke off chuckling. "And what's your name?"

"Hugh Smith."

"Well, Hugh, I'm Mrs. Kendrick, and your daddy and I were sweethearts, oh, so long ago that I can hardly believe it. We went together a long time," she mused. "Can't remember just why we broke off. Anyway, he left Decatur, and I haven't seen hide nor hair of him since. So what in the world are you doing here?"

I explained that I'd been selling Christian books in Bowie but had run out of territory and had moved to Decatur. I told her I belonged to the Seventh-day Adventist Church, and she said she'd heard of it.

"And where will you stay?" she demanded.

"Oh, I've just been walking around town looking for a place."

I wish you could have heard her, she was so excited. Really made me feel welcome. "You're coming right home with me, perfectly welcome to stay the whole time you're here. My husband's the mail carrier, and he'll be glad to have you, too. We enjoy boys, have three of our own—one just your age."

And while she was talking, she was propelling me to the depot to get my bags. There's a lot of talk today about domineering women, but I don't mind telling you I couldn't have been happier that day. It almost seemed like going home.

She put me upstairs with Teddy, her youngest, and he was just as friendly as his mom. I guess it seemed funny to him that I—a book salesman and just his age—was living away from home. He asked me a million questions and helped me out now and then.

Decatur was good territory. I went around it and other small towns in the area, and the country people were always gracious. They rarely had visitors, and summer was such a busy time that they didn't get out to town very often. It was a long way between farms— sometimes I could cut across fields—and I had to sell a book at almost every house to make it worthwhile. I talked to God while I ran or plodded along as the afternoon sun tried to broil me, and I'd tell Him about the families I'd met, ask Him to go with me and give me words to help everyone I met.

I did really well, too. Sold at about every house. In fact, the publishing men back home thought I was doing so well that they sent another boy for me to teach, Nat Billings. My good buddy, Nat, from school, and I was tickled to have him. The closer it got to September, the more homesick I got, and having Nat was almost as good as going home.

He started out going to the doors with me. I had him practice telling me about the book as we walked between houses. I thought he had it down fairly well. It seemed easy to leaf through the book and let the pictures speak for themselves. Then we came to a stretch of road with houses on both sides. The plan was that we'd each take one side then meet at the end.

Poor Nat! The sun shone hot and dry, and the wind whipped dust into our faces. When I finished, I waited around a few minutes to see if he'd come out of any of the houses within sight. It had been fun at first, waving across the road as we went, but actually I hadn't seen anything of him in over an hour or more.

We were close to town, so I decided to get a drink from the fountain in the courtyard and look around for Nat. Found him, too, sitting against a shade tree. "Boy, you finished a lot quicker than I did," I told him. "Way to go."

He mopped his forehead with a dust-stained handkerchief. "Oh, man—not quite. I had to quit, it was so hot. How can you stand it?"

I shrugged. "I don't know. It's not much different from working the farm at home."

"Besides, I'm starving to death," Nat declared. "It's after one o'clock."

I squatted down beside him. "Sounds great. I'm about famished, too. Do you want to eat here?"

His tone was flat. "I ate my lunch hours ago."

After I divided my sandwich and apple with him, Nat felt better. "Come on, go to a couple of places with me again," I told him.

"How many did you sell?" he asked, getting to his feet.

"Every place but one."

"And I sold only one," he sighed as we left the thin shade of the courtyard. "I guess I'm just not a salesman."

I laughed. "Oh, don't give up so soon. This is your first day." Then I added, "I always pray before I knock on a door." The words came out woodenly. I'd learned so much in just three months, learned that with total dependence upon God I could be a success. It was a big discovery for me, and it had changed my life, but I wasn't used to talking about it.

"Pray? Well, of course I prayed this morning," he ventured.

So I tried to explain. I told him how I felt that I was knocking on these doors because that's where God wanted me right now. I explained that I felt responsible for the people I met and that I always asked God to send the Holy Spirit to bless their reading of the books. He listened, now and then kicking a clod as we walked. Didn't say much.

Nat was beat by the end of the day. It reminded me all over again how tired I'd been those first weeks, and I felt sorry for him. But resting under trees wasn't going to sell books.

I tried not to feel exasperated with him—after all, he was my best friend—but it got so that he couldn't take it.

"I don't see how you can stand it," he moaned one afternoon. He felt so tired that he'd become cross. "This sun is about to give me heatstroke, and I'm starving. How can you miss so many meals? I'm going to pass out."

Finally we both gave up. "You sell here around the city," I suggested, "and I'll stick to the country." But he didn't sell much. And he was so homesick and hungry and tired that he went back to Keene.

I missed him, too, and felt a little mad and a whole heap sad that he hadn't made it. I turned it over and over in my mind—worrying that I'd failed him and thanking God that I'd learned the secret of being a good colporteur: depending on Him.

Chapter 9

Wild Horse

The hot, dry August days fled faster than Texas jackrabbits. I finished my Decatur territory, and Teddy Kendrick helped me fill out the notification cards. They told my customers when I'd be by with their books.

I mailed them with more misgiving than faith because I couldn't imagine how on earth I'd ever carry all those books all those miles to all those houses. Hoofing it would be impossible in the few days before I had to get back to Keene to begin school. And I didn't have a horse.

Teddy and I were still talking about the problem as we burst into the kitchen after returning from the post office. Mrs. Kendrick stood peeling potatoes. "What's the problem?" she questioned. "I just caught the tail of it."

I told her.

"We've got a mighty fast horse down in the lower pasture," she said with a little chuckle. "Use him. There's a good saddle in the barn too."

Teddy and I took the lemonade she offered us, then we went on up to our room. I was eager to check over the cartons of books I'd just gotten—books that I needed to get to the people.

My shadow stretched long under the early sun as I hiked down to look over that horse the next day. Wasps in their black and yellow striped coats dived and wheeled in the morning breeze. Far away a mockingbird sang—the notes loud in the still, clear air. A jay scolded in answer.

I gasped when I saw him. Oh, that was some magnificent horse. A tall, muscular black stallion—a little fact Mrs. Kendrick hadn't mentioned—and wilder than a maverick pony.

Slowly I sauntered up toward where he stood beside the fence. With a wild, frightened look, he pounded across the pasture and paused, panting, on the other side.

For a few minutes I just leaned there against the fence, thinking. He seemed my only chance to deliver the books, but I wondered if I could possibly tame him in time. Thursday already. I'd just have today and tomorrow to do it. Saturday, of course, I wouldn't work with him, and Sunday I'd need to sort through the orders and line everything up for delivery.

The horse still waited nervously on the other side of the field—as far away from me as possible—and munched on the short, dried grass. Glancing around, I noticed railroad tracks behind me with tall, dusty-green Johnson grass growing along them.

Pulling out my pocketknife, I cut a fair armload then brought it over to the fence. When I called to the horse, he tossed his head and rolled his eyes at me before backing farther away. So much for his eating out of my hand. Throwing the grass over the fence, I stepped aside and crouched down so he couldn't see me.

After a few minutes he cautiously approached the pile of grass and gobbled it, then galloped back to the safety of the other side of the field. Cutting more grass, I threw it over, hid, and waited for him to return and eat it.

"This could go on forever," I thought in frustration, squatting there against the thin, sharp blades. There had to be a better way. The sun was higher and hotter. Already my shirt felt glued to my back. When I heard the horse trot away, I cut just a mouthful of grass and tossed it over the fence. "Maybe that will work better," I mused. "Just a taste at a time, and I'll put it just inside the fence so he'll have to come closer."

We played that little game till afternoon. He didn't much like it, but he would finally come eat the grass while I stood nearby. I talked to him softly and tried to move slowly. The way to tame him was to make him trust me—only I didn't have much time.

At last I grabbed a handful of grass, walked over to the fence, and stood there, holding the grass out to the horse. I could tell he wanted it. "Come on, boy," I coaxed. He tossed his head. "I'm not going to hurt you." Snorting, he rolled his eyes at me, then oh, so carefully, step by step, the huge animal approached to snatch the grass from my hand.

I felt as successful as if I'd just climbed the Matterhorn. Progress! When the horse ran away with the grass, I got another bunch and waited. He eyed me for a while. I didn't move, just held out the grass and talked to him in a nice, soft voice.

"Come on, old boy. I'm not going to hurt you. I just need to ride you"—and more of the same. When I'd about given up, he took two steps forward, stretched out his neck, and took the grass. His curled lips felt soft against my hand.

We kept this up all afternoon. Eventually he stopped running away and stayed right there beside me to eat. He devoured so much, I wondered if he'd get a bellyache. I hoped not, since I had to ride him tomorrow.

Early the next morning I went to the stable for a rope and then cut across the fields. I was really praying this time. "Today's the day, Father. I need Your protection and some of Your wisdom too." The horse watched me approach—his ears flattened back—but he didn't turn and race away. I began talking soothingly to him before I got there. He eyed me a little suspiciously, I thought, but I went anyway, cut a big armload of Johnson grass, and laid it down beside me so I could feed him a mouthful at a time.

He ate out of my hand for a while, then I leaned across the fence and patted his neck with the other hand. He jumped, his skin twitching, but he kept on munching the grass, and I kept on patting and talking. After a while he seemed to enjoy it. I scratched up and down his neck, around his mane. As fast as I poked the grass over the fence, he devoured it. Finally he appeared at ease with me.

The morning went by, and the whole time I had a prayer running through the back of my mind. "Please, dear God, let me ride him today. I have to. It's my last chance."

I had earlier tied the bridle rope around my waist. Now I tried to figure out a way of getting it around his muzzle. I was already using both hands, feeding and petting him. I needed a third one desperately.

The sun climbed to the top of the sky. Our shadows huddled dark and shapeless beneath us. Then it began its slow slide to the other horizon, and I knew it was now or never. With one hand I held grass for his cavernous innards, and with the other I stopped stroking and fumblingly slipped the rope around his muzzle.

In that instant he shied and jumped, trying to get away. So I wrapped both arms around his neck, flung myself on his back, and hung on for life itself. First he reared, then leaped straight up. His hooves hit the ground with an earthshaking thud. Up and down. Again. Then again. The sky seemed to hit me between

Wild Horse

the eyes, the ground tried to pound my face. My teeth rattled, my head jerked back and forth, but I clung to him.

The dusty brown pasture grass blurred with the pale blue sky as the scared-senseless horse reared and ran and jumped. Everything I had learned about horses from growing up on a farm raced through my mind. "I've got to stay on. . . . I'd never catch him if I let go. . . . Besides, he could kill me. . . . Getting on, staying on . . . only way to break a horse is to ride him."

I have no idea how long he bucked, but after an eternity he began to slow down. Finally he came to a halt, his sides heaving, with my arms and legs still locked around him. "That's a good boy," I panted, all out of breath myself. "I'm not mad at you. We're still friends."

At last I managed to grasp the rope more securely, and I slid off him. Still talking to him, I reached down for some grass to feed him. Not for an instant did I let go of the makeshift bridle. Wrapped around his neck with a hitch over his muzzle, it permitted me to now handle him fairly well. Besides, he didn't try to get away. So I fed him some more, crooned a lot more nonsense into his ears, and we walked around the pasture until he got used to someone one third his size leading him around.

Our shadows grew longer. A breeze fanned my sweat-drenched clothes. Now I stared at the pasture gate with misgivings. In the shelter of the fence the horse had quieted down. But did I dare open the gate? If he bolted, he could drag me on the end of the rope all the way into town. We circled the pasture again, stopping now and then so he could eat. As we came to the gate I stopped. The stallion paused too.

The sky seemed an upside-down blue bowl covering the countryside. Not a cloud anywhere. In the distance, faint hills faded into the horizon. The sun hung a few feet above the rim of the earth, and for the first time all day I realized how empty my stomach felt.

Holding the rope loosely in my left hand, I put the other on the gate latch. "Please, Father," I whispered, looking at the sky, "don't let him get scared." I pressed the latch and gave the gate a big shove. The huge horse whinnied and nuzzled at my back. For a second I wished I'd thought to bring some carrots or sugar, then remembered I hadn't because I didn't want anyone to know what I planned to do.

"Come on, big boy, we'll have something good at the house." Taking two steps forward, I tugged gently at the rope. He followed. So I walked through the gate and across the field. That huge black stallion followed like a little lamb. Well . . . almost, anyway.

"We'll get a saddle on you, fellow," I told him, "then see how you take to being ridden."

A rabbit streaked in front of us. The horse snorted but didn't miss a step. On we went, slowly, gently, right up to the house. Mrs. Kendrick had just stepped outside to throw some vegetable peelings to the chickens. When she saw us, she screamed, threw her apron over her face, and ran into the house.

"Hugh! Hugh!" she called out the window. "Stop right where you are! You hear me?"

Afraid she'd scare the horse, I stopped. "It's all right; he's my friend," I protested.

"Oh, no, no! What would your daddy say?" she cried. "He'd never forgive me if I let anything happen to you."

I brought the horse a little closer to the house, where I wouldn't need to shout. "All I want is a saddle so I can try riding him. You said——"

"Oh, no!" She was actually crying. "Listen, he's a

Wild Horse

killer. Not six months ago he trampled a man to death." Terror filled her eyes, and I felt sorry to have upset her, and shocked, too, at what she said.

"Mrs. Kendrick, you told me I could use him."

"Oh, I was only joking. You should know me by now. I was joking."

"But he's tame as a puppy. See?" I said. "May I lead him to the stable?"

She nodded, unable to say a word.

The horse didn't seem to mind my saddling him, and he didn't object when I climbed up on his high back. Then I rode him into the yard. Mrs. Kendrick stood just outside the door. "Oh, Hugh!" she exclaimed. "Your guardian angel sure has been busy."

"See, I've got me a good, tame riding pony," I told her. "He loves me." We cantered around the yard, then I let him take me into the pasture for a little run. He raced along like the wind, and I knew I'd deliver my books in record time.

And I did. Sometimes we'd stop so I could give him corn or let him drink. But mostly we flew down the road between farms and towns, and I'd seldom been happier.

I took the train back home as soon as I'd finished deliveries. Just before I left I bought Mrs. Kendrick a box of chocolate candy—her favorite—as a sort of thank you for all she'd done. Not having a chance to give it to her before I left, I put it on a shelf where she'd be sure to find it.

Four years later—during camp meeting—I heard a knock on the front door. When I called, "Come on in," Mrs. Kendrick rushed in at me, her arms outstretched. She gave me a crushing hug, then held me out at arm's length.

"I want you to know that you've made a Christian out of me," she enthused, tears glistening. "I read all those books you left, and I want to be a Christian." Her words gushed up like a spring. "I'm at camp meeting to be baptized, and you're the reason. Hugh, you're the one who got me started. Are you going to watch?"

Feeling tears suspiciously close to my own eyelids, I replied, "I wouldn't miss it for anything."

"It's funny about old people," Lisey mused. She sat in the den ripping out a granny square that didn't meet her approval, rolling the blue yarn loosely around the skein.

"How so?" her mother asked.

"Well, I've been thinking of all the neat stories Mr. Smith tells about when he was a kid. People had a different kind of fun back then, didn't they?" She picked up her crochet hook and began to chain again.

"They lived differently, that's so," Mother agreed. "But I think that basic problems stay the same. Mr. Smith was working to earn money for academy, just like you're doing. You both want an education from the type of school that stresses the Bible as the basis of your life's philosophy." She dusted the last figurine on the mantel, then crossed the room to begin on the bookcases.

Lisey clipped the first round of the granny square and picked up another skein to tie on. "Grandma said I should ask you about a Mary somebody. An old lady?"

"Mary Moore! She was an elderly lady who lived in the same apartment complex as your daddy and I when we were first married."

"Well?"

"Oh, just a rather special lady. She'd done a bit of writing and teaching, and she could tell the most marvelous stories." Mother stopped dusting, a faraway look on her face. "She had the comfortable, dumpy figure

Wild Horse

that a lot of older ladies get, and I got a kick out of something she told me one of the first times we visited."

"What's that?"

"She laughed at how vain she'd been about her eighteen-inch waist when she was a young woman."

"Eighteen inches! Wow." Lisey frowned at her work. "Is this Mary Moore still alive?"

"Oh, no. She was in her mid-seventies when we met. But the last time I heard from her———" Mother's voice faded. "I'll never forget it. She'd moved away to live with a lady who could help take care of her—she'd gotten feeble.

"But we still exchanged Christmas letters. That year she sent her notes out early, and she wrote something like this to me: 'I'm feeling so tired lately. I'll see you when Jesus comes.' She died before the holidays."

Lisey blinked in sympathy. "How awfully sad!"

"Well, yes. But she just went to sleep—resting in Jesus' love. Anyway," she went on briskly, "what I wanted to tell you is that she had quite a time at her first job. She was a live-in schoolteacher for an extremely wealthy family. Since you've been collecting old-fashioned stories this summer, are you interested?"

"You just keep telling, and I'll keep crocheting," Lisey laughed.

"OK. Here goes . . ."

Chapter 10

Gift of Love

Mary Moore—dressed in a crisp linen blouse and sleek black skirt—looked at her reflection mirrored in the glass pane of the railroad coach window. "First impressions are important," she thought. "I must look neat, since I surely won't be as well dressed as Mrs. Albertson."

"Albertson . . . Albertson . . . Albertson," the train's clicking wheels seemed to chant. "Albertson . . . Roselawn . . . Albertson . . . Roselawn." Closing her eyes, Mary tried to picture the wealthy Mrs. Josephine Albertson, mistress of Roselawn Estate.

"This is really different from the plans I had for myself," she thought, and a frown creased her face. "Being a live-in schoolteacher to four children is really a contrast to teaching English grammar and literature to a hundred or more academy and college students."

Mary had graduated from college just three months earlier. However, poor health had prevented her from accepting any of the choice positions offered her by different schools that year. But while resting up from the stress of final exams and graduation, she prayed that God would show her what to do with her life. Then one day she received a letter from her college president.

"We have been contacted by a Mrs. Josephine Albertson in California," he wrote. "She asked whether we had any student who would be willing to teach at a small school on her estate. There will be four students—her twin daughters, a crippled girl whom she has taken into her home, and the son of her chauffeur and estate manager. Mrs. Albertson thought we might know a young woman who would like living in southern California because of its healthful climate. I immediately thought of you," the letter concluded.

To Mary it seemed a God-given opportunity to regain her health and still make money to pay off her school loans. It was a real answer to prayer. A few weeks later, in the fall of 1914, she was on the Santa Fe train and westward bound.

"Po-mo-na!" The conductor's foghorn voice blared into her thoughts. "Po-mo-na, next sto-op!"

Mary got down a small travel case from the rack above her head, pulled on immaculate white gloves, then peered out the dusty window for Mrs. Albertson's chauffeur. He was to meet her.

Huffing and puffing, the train squealed and shuddered to a stop, and travelers poured down its steps amid clouds of steam. At last the crowd sorted itself into couples and families that went away together, leaving Mary standing alone. A youngish man came toward her, stopped, and tipped his hat. "Miss Mary Moore?"

"Yes, sir." She let out a small sigh of relief. "I've come to teach at Roselawn."

"I'm Mr. Fredericks, Mrs. Albertson's chauffeur." He nodded toward her travel case. "Is that all the luggage you have?"

"All for now. My trunk will come later."

He grinned. "Never yet saw a lady who could put all her finery into such a small box. Shall we go?"

Mary followed him, but his remark nibbled at the worry she'd pushed back into a corner of her mind.

"Finery," he'd said. College had been one round after another of tuition and doctor bills. Through her college years she had enlivened her meager wardrobe by new buttons, a new collar, or the new gloves she now wore, but not by many new clothes.

How would a person who had lived simply and frugally all her life fit into a five-thousand-acre estate like Roselawn? How would she get along with her employer? Would the woman be snobbish because of her wealth and position? "Will I be envious of her and her money?" Mary wondered.

The car turned down a tree-lined drive and finally stopped before a great white house. "It's beautiful," Mary thought. "Absolutely beautiful!" Surely every flower that bloomed in California grew in profusion in the gardens surrounding the house.

The chauffeur opened her door. Head held high, Mary strode up the brightly bordered walk to the large front door. Mrs. Albertson opened it. "Miss Mary—at last!" she greeted her. "Welcome to Roselawn!"

Mary extended her hand, and the woman held it for a moment in both of hers while she looked into Mary's blue eyes. "We're so happy to have you, so thankful to have a Christian teacher for our children."

Mary returned the smile, her glance taking in Mrs. Albertson's appearance. The woman's blonde hair was piled atop her head. A well-made but simple dress set off a plump figure. "Why, she's nothing like what I feared," Mary mused. "She's not severe or haughty or overdressed. Instead, she's just pleasant and—well, a lady. And she couldn't be more than a year older than I am."

"You must be exhausted from your trip," Mrs. Albertson said. "Let me show you to your room, and you can freshen up a bit before dinner."

Mary followed her up the high stairway, down a hall,

and into a large apartment. "This is the sitting room," the woman told her with a wave of her hand, "and this will be your bedroom."

"It's lovely," Mary breathed, not adding that it was the first time she'd actually seen wall-to-wall carpeting. "It—it's so big. I hardly expected anything like this when you said I'd have my own room. It's wonderful!"

Mrs. Albertson smiled at the young teacher's pleasure. "Actually it's the guest room," she told her. "But we have few guests, what with my husband's illness and all. I felt that you would like a private place that you could call your own after teaching all day."

"Oh, thank you," Mary said, crossing to the open porch that held her bed. "The view is just beautiful."

"You'll need a quiet place to work on your lessons, anyway," Mrs. Albertson added. "And by the way, you'll meet the children at dinner time."

Mary met the whole household that evening. The children, the chauffeur, the maid—they all ate together at the long table. The young teacher couldn't get over her employer's lack of snobbishness. "Who would think she'd eat with the hired help?" she thought. "I always heard that rich people ate alone, that they didn't socialize with their workers."

Before many weeks passed, Mary realized that although her mistress presided over a multimillion-dollar estate, she was an extremely lonely woman. Her story came out in bits and pieces of conversation—fragments that Mary put together to learn the whole of her loneliness.

The illness that had made her much older husband an invalid had also destroyed his mind. He was little more than a child who needed constant attention. Before the man became housebound, he spent every day in the nearby small town, and the people there took advantage

Gift of Love

of his weakened mind. If he went into a restaurant and ordered a sandwich, he might hand the cashier a ten dollar bill. "Here's your change, Mr. Albertson," he or she might say, putting a quarter into his outstretched hand. Since his reasoning abilities were almost gone, Mr. Albertson wouldn't know the difference.

When his wife finally realized how the townspeople were cheating her and her husband, she established charge accounts for him with every store in the area. That way she would see a ticket for each item he bought and would know if someone had charged him twenty dollars for a package of cotton handkerchiefs or five dollars for a bag of gumdrops. Needless to say, she became unpopular with those who had swindled her husband.

Even the people of her church tried to take advantage of her, she confided to Mary. "It's a privilege to pay tithe and to give to missions or to help out in our welfare program. But the church members seem to think that just because we do have money, we should throw it around on the most insignificant things. And they get angry if I question the need."

Teacher and mistress of the estate became quite close, probably because Mary accepted her for herself, not for her wealth. Far from being envious, Mary decided that money brought more problems than it solved.

She enjoyed living at Roselawn, liked teaching the children, and loved the sunny climate. As December drew near she looked forward to visiting her brother in Los Angeles and imagined his surprise at how much her health had improved.

When the two friends went into Pomona in late November, Mary happily pointed out the Christmas decorations already brightening the town. For a moment Mrs. Albertson didn't answer. When she did, it was with such bitterness in her voice that Mary stopped short to stare at her. "I just *hate* Christmas!"

"Hate Christmas?" With the swiftness of a firefly's flicker, Mary's childhood Christmas memories flashed through her mind. Her family, always poor, had had little money with which to celebrate the holiday. But there had been secrets and presents lovingly made or bought and hidden away. "Why do you say that?" she asked, her voice low.

Mrs. Albertson shook her head. "Perhaps I shouldn't have said it. But I can't help feeling that way."

"Your husband . . ." Mary began.

"Oh, no." She paused. "The truth is, Mary, that everybody I know, people who don't even speak to me the year round, send me the cheapest, most trivial bit of junk they can buy and add a note saying that they hope I like their gift and have a merry Christmas."

Mary still didn't understand. "But why?"

"Because I have the money to purchase something expensive for them. Because then I will be obligated to buy them something in return."

"I can't imagine anyone . . ." Mary's voice trailed off in disbelief.

"Oh, I try to make it happy for the children," Mrs. Albertson said. "But I'm always immensely relieved when the whole ordeal is over. I'm put in such a bad position, I never really know what to do."

That night Mary lay awake, thinking of Mrs. Albertson's words. "What could I possibly get her that she wouldn't consider cheap?" the schoolteacher wondered. "She pays me well for the work I do here, but what with paying off school bills, I hardly have enough money to buy a few inexpensive things for my family."

The days passed, and she still pondered what to buy. At last she decided she would only write her a note that

Gift of Love

expressed her appreciation for everything she'd done for her. She wouldn't presume to purchase a gift for someone who had everything.

Two weeks before Christmas Mary sat in her room tatting, relaxing after a long day. Working with her hands always helped unknot her nerves. Creating something intricately pretty from simple thread seemed to give her a new perspective on her daily problems. Now looking at the delicate pattern of the doily she had tatted, she remembered a comment Mrs. Albertson had made to the cook as the woman cleared the table.

The cook had taken the linen table napkins and laid them on the sideboard in the dining room. Before the invention of paper napkins, people used cloth ones at each meal for a couple of days, and naturally each person tried to get his own for each meal.

"I wish I knew some way of marking napkins so I could tell which one went to which person," Mrs. Albertson had said. "Surely there must be some way to mark them so we wouldn't always have the problem of who got whose napkin."

"I could tat napkin rings," Mary mused. "If I laced a different color ribbon through each one, then each person could remember his own by the colored ribbon around it."

So, using white thread, she made strips of tatting several inches long, one for each person who sat at the table. Then she bought ribbons and laced one through each strip so that he or she could tie the ribbon in a bow around the napkin.

Still fearing that she'd made a cheap, worthless gift that would insult her friend, Mary didn't have the nerve to give it to her in person. Instead, she wrapped it, enclosed a loving note, and left it in a place where Mrs. Albertson would find it after Mary had gone.

As she left the house Mrs. Albertson handed her a brightly papered package.

Mary's misgivings about her inexpensive homemade present intensified when at Christmas she opened the box. It held enough pale-blue wool material to make a long, full skirt. In addition it contained matching blue silk for a blouse. She gasped as she fingered the rich cloths. "How can I ever look at Mrs. Albertson again?" she wondered in panic. "I've never had anything this nice. What will she think of my gift to her?"

Mrs. Albertson was with a sister when she opened the little box the teacher had left behind. As she read the note and her fingers touched the delicate handwork and dainty ribbons her eyes filled with tears.

"What's the matter?" her sister asked. "What on earth is the matter?"

"This dear girl," the mistress of Roselawn said, tears still spilling down her cheeks. "This dear, thoughtful girl. I didn't know there was a soul in the world who thought enough of me to take the time and effort to make something for me with her own hands."

Chapter 11

Weekend of Terror

"Here's the letter I've been waiting for," Josephine Albertson commented as she opened the pale-pink envelope she held.

"From your aunt and cousin?" Mary Moore asked.

Mrs. Albertson nodded as she read. "You know, I've spent so much time tracking them down that it's really a thrill to finally hear from them. Somehow we lost contact with them over the years. After they left the church, they seemed to disappear."

"Were they pleased to hear from you?"

"Oh, yes. It's such a friendly letter." Mrs. Albertson placed the envelope in her desk drawer. "In fact, they seem as eager to come spend a weekend with me as I am to have them."

Within a few weeks the visit was arranged. Mrs. Albertson's relatives would stay in Mary's room—the guest room—for the weekend, and she would go see her brother in Los Angeles. On the Friday afternoon that they came, Mr. Fredericks took Mary to the train station, then picked up the two women, who had arrived at nearly the same time. Mary, of course, could have no idea of the excitement that was going to happen at Roselawn during her absence.

Mrs. Albertson waited at the front window, watching for her car to return. At last it rolled slowly up the long driveway and stopped in front of the wide walk. She opened the door before they could knock.

"Aunt Kathryn, Cousin Meg, how wonderful to see you!" She embraced each woman, then held her at arm's length.

"You look wonderful," she said, noting their sweeping dresses, their elaborate coiffures, their gaily flowered hats. They had become even more style-conscious than when she had last seen them. "Please come in." The women followed her into the entryway, through the curtained arch, and into the parlor.

"Roselawn Estate"—Aunt Kathryn savored the words—"it's as beautiful as its name." She sat down in an intricately carved, brocade-covered chair. "Now tell us about yourself."

"Please do, Josie," Meg echoed. "We were so surprised to get your letter. I remember playing with you as a child, but . . . how did you find us?"

Mrs. Albertson smiled. "I've always wondered what happened to you folks. Grandma thought that you'd moved to California, and after I'd settled down out here, you were in my thoughts more and more. Finally I began asking around in the family and, well, at last I found you." She leaned forward. "Wouldn't you like some lemonade? We have some made up."

"Sounds wonderful," Aunt Kathryn replied, pulling off her long gloves. "The train was so hot. If we opened the windows, cinders blew in and covered us, and if we kept them closed——" She shuddered slightly.

". . . we were practically steamed alive," Meg finished her mother's sentence.

Mrs. Albertson left the room and returned with a silver tray, a tall moisture-beaded pitcher of lemonade, and three ice-filled glasses. Setting the tray down on a low marble table, she poured the sweet-sour drink before speaking. "Do you ever have a chance to attend the Adventist church?" she inquired, handing a frosty glass to her aunt.

Taking a sip, Aunt Kathryn shook her head. "Actually, that was part of our break with the family. Theodore, bless his soul, couldn't abide the rigidity of the church doctrines and standards."

"He loved for Mamma to dress fancy," Meg giggled, accepting a glass from her cousin. "He always said he wished he could drape her in diamonds and pearls."

Nodding, Mrs. Albertson said nothing.

"Anyway, after Theo moved out here because of his job, and we were away from family pressure to attend church, we naturally stopped going. Mamma and Grandma were so upset that, well, somehow I just couldn't bear writing to them and getting their letters saying that they were praying for me." She gave a slight shrug of her ruffled shoulder. "But, dear Josie, I'm so happy that you found us. I have missed my family."

Mrs. Albertson smiled again. "I'm pleased that I've been able to contact you again. You, Meg, were a favorite playmate of mine. And you, Auntie, were always so much fun to be around. I always looked forward to spending the day at your house." She picked up the pitcher. "More lemonade?"

"About half a glass," Meg answered. "Have to watch my waistline. But this is delicious."

"Please, the same for me," Aunt Kathryn added. "The train trip was torture."

Josephine Albertson poured and talked. "You know, as a teenager, I went out of the church myself. God's restrictions—as I considered His law—were just too much for me. But then I came to a crisis in my life, to a place where death seemed the only way out."

Her cousin put out her hand, touching Mrs. Albertson's arm. "Why, no, dear Josie. Whatever for?"

She shook her head. "The reason isn't important. What does matter is that I found Christ, really found Him, for the first time in my life. And I discovered that what I had considered restrictions weren't that at all, but only guides to help me *live* in the fullest extent of the word."

Aunt Kathryn smiled sympathetically. "Of course, we all must find our own solutions to our problems."

"Truthfully, if I had not found Christ and accepted His gift of love for me, I wouldn't be sitting before you now. I've found joy in being a Christian that I didn't know was possible." She stood up. "But I'm being very inconsiderate of you. You must be weary from your trip. Let me take you to your room. Mr. Fredericks has already taken your bags."

The two women followed her up the long stairway and down the hall to Mary's room. Mrs. Albertson showed them where to put their things and left them, saying that dinner would be served in an hour.

After dinner the three women gathered with the children in the parlor for Friday evening worship. Aunt Kathryn and Meg sat quietly, if a little bored, while Mrs. Albertson read from the Bible. Then the children said their favorite Bible verses. After a few songs they knelt to pray, and then the children went to bed.

"That was sweet," Aunt Kathryn remarked as the children left the room. "I mean the earnest way they say those Bible verses."

"I guess John 3:16 was the first verse I learned," Meg added, a faraway look in her eyes.

"But we do go to church now," Aunt Kathryn said after a moment. "In fact, in just the past few years we've discovered the most amazing things. You may find it hard to believe, but we'd love to share them with you."

Weekend of Terror 99

Meg leaned forward. "There are *other dimensions* in this world that most people know nothing about!"

"Or else they refuse to accept them," Aunt Kathryn interjected. "Some find it hard to believe, and others are simply frightened by phenomena they do not understand."

"Are you speaking of spiritualism?" Mrs. Albertson asked.

"Then you have heard of it!" her aunt gushed. "Isn't it marvelous? Isn't it comforting to know that death is not the end of life!"

After a fleeting second of silence, Mrs. Albertson replied, "I, too, know that death is not the end of life—especially for those who accept Christ as their Saviour. But I believe the Bible description of life after death. In 1 Corinthians 15 Paul spends nearly sixty verses describing death as man's enemy and as caused by his sin. He finished the chapter with words of man's triumph over death through Christ's life on earth, His death, and resurrection."

She paused to look into the eyes of her listeners. "He writes that we shall not all sleep—that is, sleep in death—but that we shall be changed in a moment's time when Jesus comes. 'For the trumpet shall sound, and the dead shall be raised incorruptible,' is the way Paul put it."

"I'm sure he meant well," Aunt Kathryn said gently, "but we have so much greater knowledge now. We realize that when we go into that state most people call death, we are not really gone. We have just entered another phase of our life."

" 'Ye shall not surely die.' Why that was the first lie that Satan told Eve!" her niece exclaimed. "How do you discount the words of Ecclesiastes 9:5: 'The living know that they shall die: but the dead know not any thing'?"

"Of course, it's hard to know what part of the Bible to take literally," Meg murmured. "If you could have seen what we've heard and seen!" She threw up her hands in a gesture of amazement. "You just wouldn't believe the experiences we've had."

"That's true," her mother nodded. "A person who hasn't experienced contact with those who still exist—though not in this realm—just can't imagine the thrill and wonder of it all."

"What kind of contact have you had?" Mrs. Albertson asked. "Séances?"

"Oh, yes, and they are exciting," Meg bubbled. "Why, we've seen people reunited with members of their families who have passed on. We've seen them hold each other and weep with joy."

Mrs. Albertson gasped. "Meg, Aunt Kathryn, you're dabbling with the evil spirits themselves. You're inviting evil angels into your lives."

"You wouldn't say that if you'd seen what we've witnessed," Meg told her seriously. "Why, the joy of a person who's been contacted by a friend from the other side! There's nothing evil about it. It's, well—just beautiful."

Putting out her hand for silence, Mrs. Albertson leaned forward. "Pardon me. I thought I heard one of the children in the hall." They resumed talking a few minutes longer, then she paused again. "I'm sure I heard them. Lois?" she called. "Is that you?"

No reply. But she could hear definite sounds of footsteps walking down the hall, even though she could see no one. Aunt Kathryn got up. "Josie, dear, the children are in bed, and we're all in the parlor." She stepped to the door and looked down the hall. Cocking her head to one side, she listened. The footsteps became louder, but no one was there.

Meg said solemnly, "I believe that someone is trying to contact us."

"You mean——!" Mrs. Albertson exclaimed.

"Don't be frightened, dear. They don't hurt anyone. Obviously they heard us talking about them and wanted to come for a little visit."

"Has this happened before? I mean to you folks?" Mrs. Albertson tried to control the rising tremble in her voice.

"Oh, yes. Why we've——" her voice stopped as the lights in the room went out.

"Is this—I mean, do they affect the lights?" she inquired.

"They can be playful," Aunt Kathryn replied indulgently. "Almost like a naughty child."

"It doesn't have to be 'them,' " Meg said, "though, of course, it might be. I mean, it could be a blown fuse or something. Then again, maybe they want some attention."

"Well, I'll get some candles. They're right in the kitchen." Mrs. Albertson stood up, bumped her leg on the end table—and the lights came on.

"I guess it was a fuse," Aunt Kathryn laughed.

Her niece tried to laugh, too, not mentioning that the light shining brightly now beside the organ had not been on before.

Meg smiled at her cousin. "I'm afraid we're scaring dear Josie."

"You never have told us why you came to California," Aunt Kathryn said, changing the subject.

They talked for a while longer. At last Mrs. Albertson stood up to go, explaining that for her, Sabbath was a day to rise early. She invited her guests to go to church, but they declined, insisting that they'd sleep in and then take a walk around the grounds. As she went to bed she wondered what she'd gotten herself into. She read her Bible a little longer than usual and prayed more intensely for God's protection. Several times she woke up to hear "those" footsteps.

Sabbath passed uneventfully. As the sun went down and darkness enveloped the mansion and invaded the spacious rooms, evil seemed to permeate the whole house. The estate family gathered in the parlor for popcorn and games. They were all present: Mrs. Albertson and her children, Mr. Fredericks and his son, Aunt Kathryn, Meg, and the maid. And above the sound of their talk and laughter one could hear voices—high, bubbling voices—away in other parts of the house. First in one room and then another the voices muttered and echoed and laughed.

Mrs. Albertson tried to ignore the strange noises. She prayed silently, and for the children's sake she didn't mention what she heard. But she asked Mr. Fredericks to accompany her when she went to the kitchen. "Have you heard anything?" she whispered.

He nodded. "Do you think it's what you mentioned this afternoon?"

She shuddered. "It must be. What can we do?"

"Nothing, I guess, but pray."

"Put a few candles in your pocket, please," she whispered. "And matches."

Nodding wordlessly, he stuffed his pockets with some red candles. "I'd hate to frighten the children," he murmured as they returned to the living room.

The evening went on, but it was not what one would call a success. Footsteps ran over squeaky boards in other parts of the house. Voices continued to flit from room to room. Then the lights went out again. Meg gave a little squeal in the darkness.

"Hush!" her mother commanded. "There's nothing

to be frightened of. They never hurt people."

"Mamma, what does she mean?" Viva, one of the children, asked.

"Oh, nothing, darling—nothing I can explain right now." Mrs. Albertson patted the girl on the shoulder. Mr. Fredericks lighted the candles and handed them to the children, who giggled at the grotesque shadows they cast against the wallpaper of the darkened room. Then the lights flicked back on again in the parlor and other areas of the house.

That night Mr. Fredericks slept with his son. Mrs. Albertson crowded the three girls into one room and then dozed in the room next to them. All through the night the voices and footsteps continued. She hardly slept at all, getting only a few fitful hours in before dawn.

When she awakened and saw the time, she rushed into the kitchen, expecting to find her guests fully dressed and waiting for breakfast. Instead she found them in their robes. They were drinking Postum that they had prepared and were talking quietly. As much as they hated to admit it, they were afraid too.

"I hardly understand it," Meg told her mother. "You know, I've always been exhilarated by my experiences with them. But there were so many things happening at once. What with the lights going on and off all night and hearing 'people' stomping up and down the hall and then laughing in the same room with us, I hardly slept a wink all night."

"I feel the same way," her mother replied. "And, Josie, I'm embarrassed at the way these ... spirits ... are acting." She gave a forced laugh. "But I don't know what to do with them."

Mrs. Albertson shook her head without answering. Although she'd prayed, it hadn't seemed to help much.

Her sleepless nights, combined with the fear that gripped her heart like an iron hand, had left her almost too exhausted to talk. Pushing herself up from the table, she managed to say, "What can I get you for breakfast? eggs? hotcakes?"—she swallowed past the lump in her throat—"oatmeal and cream? Our cows give rich cream."

"Oh, please—nothing for me," Aunt Kathryn told her. "This hot drink tastes good. Just as good as coffee," she added.

"I'll just take some toast and your freshly churned butter," Meg said graciously. "But let me fix it myself. You look tired."

The happy day that Mrs. Albertson had planned with such anticipation didn't quite come off. Her nerves taut, she jumped at any strange noise and dreaded the coming of night. Sunday night was even worse than the other two evenings. She lay awake all night as she prayed and repeated Bible promises to herself. And through all the long, dark hours, she heard the loud footsteps, the patter of running feet, the high and low voices. The lights constantly flickered off and on as the unseen presences flipped the switches.

Somewhat shaken, Aunt Kathryn and Meg refused breakfast Monday morning. Hurriedly they left with Mr. Fredericks for the Santa Fe station. He put them on the train, then met the oncoming one. Mary got off, light-hearted from her short vacation. She chatted away until she noticed that the chauffeur was unusually quiet.

Mrs. Albertson met her at the door. "Mary, come right in and sit down." The words tumbled over each other. "You can't begin teaching until I tell you the ordeal I've—we've—been through this weekend."

Mary took a long look at her friend. "You look exhausted," she exclaimed. "Whatever is the matter?"

"I hardly know where to begin. My Aunt Kathryn and cousin Meg are Spiritualists."

"You mean they believe in the dead talking with them?"

"Something like that. Evil spirits filled this house all the time they were here. We've had lights going on and off and heard voices and footsteps from rooms in the house where there was no one. It began Friday night and got worse every night." She buried her face in her hands and let her tears of fright and frustration come. "I've prayed, but you can't imagine what it's been like. I just don't know what to do."

Speechless, Mary sat down beside her. She put her arm around her and gave her a clean handkerchief from her purse. At last Mrs. Albertson raised her head. "What are you going to do about it?" she asked.

Mary looked at her. "What do you mean?" the schoolteacher wanted to know.

"These evil angels have been in this house, and their mediums have actually been living in your room. What are you going to do about it? Where are you going to sleep?"

"In my own bed, of course!"

"But you can't! I mean, how can you stay in that room when for the past three nights those evil spirits have been doing such strange things? Aren't you afraid?" She stared at Mary with terror in her eyes.

Mary sat up a little straighter and spoke clearly. "No. I have no intention of giving over *my* room to the devil. It's mine, and I expect the Lord and His angels to drive the spirits out. More than that, there's no reason why the devil and his angels should live in this house."

Mrs. Albertson studied her face, and hope began to creep into her own. "You mean——?"

"We know that God is much more powerful than the

devil. So we'll ask Him to expel Satan and fill this house with good angels."

The two friends talked for a long time, Mary trying to comfort and relieve Mrs. Albertson's fears. Then they knelt together and prayed for care and protection and for God to drive the evil from Roselawn. Getting up, Mrs. Albertson, her voice shaking with emotion, said, "I don't care if they are my relatives. They'll never set foot in this house again!"

Mary called the children, and they went to the little schoolhouse for the day's work. All through the day she sent prayers heavenward. That night, after studying her Sabbath School lesson and praying, Mary gave herself into God's care and went to bed. She halfway expected some manifestations of the evil ones Mrs. Albertson had described so vividly, but the night passed without incident. She did keep waking up fitfully, however.

She thought of the words of Psalm 91:11: "He shall give his angels charge over thee, to keep thee in all thy ways." And then she would sleep again. Repeatedly she jerked awake to pray and claim the promise of Psalm 34:7: "The angel of the Lord encampeth round about them that fear him, and delivereth them." So she awakened and slept and awakened and slept until dawn brought sunlight into her room.

Dressing quickly, she went downstairs to find Mrs. Albertson. "How did you sleep?" she asked her. "Did you hear anything?"

"Not a thing. I was up and down all night, but I heard nothing at all. I heard nothing and saw nothing anywhere in the house."

Mary smiled and gave her friend a little hug. "We serve a mighty and wonderful God, don't we?"

"Oh, don't we!" Mrs. Albertson agreed.

Chapter 12

Right Angles and a Prayer

As autumn passed into winter and winter melted into spring, Mary enjoyed her position at Roselawn more and more. All of Josephine Albertson's employees seemed like one congenial family, working *with* Mrs. Albertson more than for her. However, Mary had one problem, which she did her best to avoid.

The hired help at Roselawn, while most were quite intelligent, were not well-educated. Because Mary had a college degree her co-workers assumed that she thought herself superior to them. If she made an innocent remark that someone knew to be incorrect, they were certain to laugh and say, "Oh, our Miss College Education is speaking." Or if she showed her knowledge in any one of many different areas, someone was sure to sneer, "Listen, everybody. Miss College Education is telling us something."

One dark autumn evening she stood in the moonlight behind the main house. Gazing at the diamond-studded sky, she could pick out several different constellations. Intent with her observing, she didn't notice one of the other employees come up until the woman stood in back of her. "What are you doing out here all alone?" she asked.

"Just enjoying the beauty of the night," Mary said. "I like to see how many constellations I can find."

The woman looked at her in disbelief. "You have no idea what a fool I think you are!"

Mary quickly learned not to parade her knowledge, not to appear to know anything that those around her thought she should know nothing about. Having a quick mind and a sharp wit, she found it hard to bite back words that could bring ridicule. But she managed to do it to avoid embarrassing herself and antagonizing others. She learned to think twice before she spoke, learned not to mention anything that others would consider too "educated."

As spring arrived the children became excited at the prospect of a tennis court that Mrs. Albertson promised to put on the estate grounds. There was much talk about it at the dinner table, much discussion as to the fine points of the game of tennis. The children especially stressed the exercise benefits of tennis, how it would develop their arm muscles and teach them to run fast and stop quickly.

Mrs. Albertson decided to put the court in as economically as possible. Instead of hiring construction workers to lay the cement, she asked her yardmen to do it. Mr. Fredericks, her chauffeur, would supervise the project.

The teacher watched and listened with interest as the project developed from the talk stage to actual work. She was interested in how Mr. Fredericks would handle the job. He was an unusual man, she thought. Though he had practically no formal education, he was highly intelligent, and his son was every bit as smart. But his lack of education made him feel inferior to her, she guessed, because at the slightest opportunity he would make some sarcastic remark concerning her college degree.

She stood at her desk, teaching, on the morning that work on the tennis court would begin when she heard a

Right Angles and a Prayer

knock outside. "Excuse me, children," she said and turned to answer the classroom door. Opening it, she discovered Mr. Fredericks, hat in hand, with a strange look on his face.

"Yes?" she asked. "Does Mrs. Albertson need something?"

The man just stood there.

"Please come in."

He stepped inside the room, closing the door with a bang. For a moment he stood looking at the cheerful classroom. Bouquets of flowers stood on Mary's desk and on the windowsills. The back wall and the space above the blackboard displayed samples of the students' art and classwork. A breeze flitted through the screened windows of the little schoolhouse, fluttering the papers on the teacher's desk.

"Yes? What can I do for you?"

The chauffeur seemed to look straight through her. No one could miss the contempt in his face and voice as he inquired, "Is there anything in that so-called college education of yours to show you how to lay out an exact right angle for the corners of the tennis court?"

Mr. Fredericks continued to stare at her. The children watched, their faces holding both trust in her ability and wonder at the man's words. Mary knew that if she couldn't answer the challenge that moment both Mr. Fredericks and the students would discount her as a teacher. How could she continue to instruct her pupils if she had lost their respect? But math and science were not her strong points, since she had been an English major in college.

A smirk playing around his lips, Mr. Fredericks gazed down at her. The children, confident, yet questioning, looked at her. Mary closed her eyes for an instant to send an emergency message to the main campus of the University of Heaven. Without help she knew she could not answer.

Like a flash of light, the thought came: The solution lies in the field of geometry. Then a second thought: Remember the theorem that says the sum of the squares of two sides of a right triangle is equal to the square of the hypotenuse.

Mary smiled. "Thank You, God," she thought. "And now, please, I need to find two figures that multiplied by themselves and added would give a simple number from which one could easily get the square root, and this would be the third side of the triangle." She sent another SOS to heaven. Just as quickly the answer came, as if someone were writing the words in her mind:

Six times six equals thirty-six.

Eight times eight equals sixty-four.

Thirty-six plus sixty-four equals one hundred.

One hundred is ten times ten.

Almost casually she remarked to Mr. Fredericks, "I suppose you know exactly where you want the corner of the tennis court?"

"Of course I do."

"Then drive a stake there and tie a string to it. Lay the string in the general direction you want the first side to go. Measure off six feet and put a stake there."

"All right. But——"

"Now take the string and lay it in the general direction you want the other side of the court to go. Measure off eight feet and place a stake there."

The children watched and listened proudly, nodding to one another. They had known that she could do it.

"Now, measure between the two end stakes," Mary continued. "Move them back and forth until the distance between them is exactly ten feet. When you've

Right Angles and a Prayer

done that, the corner formed by the triangle you've made will be an exact right angle."

He nodded. "Yes, ma'am."

She smiled. "Just do the same thing for each of the four corners of the court."

The expression of astonished respect on his face was something to see. Fumblingly putting on his hat, he mumbled a thank you and left the room.

That night as Mary knelt beside her bed she prayed, "You've always helped me with my big problems. But today You helped me recall something that I hardly remember learning. Dear Lord, You actually put the words I needed right into my mouth."

Later Mary read a reference to what carpenters call the "six-eight-ten" rule for laying out right angles. She smiled to herself as she remembered the look on Mr. Fredericks' face. And again she sent up a quick thank You to the One who knows everything—even the mathematical equation to establish a right angle!

Chapter 13

The Ungrateful Cow

"I'm going to ride over to the nursery today with Mr. Fredericks and the yardmen to get some shrubbery," Mrs. Albertson told Mary one morning.

"I'll look after things," Mary said.

"You don't know what a relief it is to have you take care of Roselawn when I'm away. Before you came, well, I just never went anywhere that I couldn't take the children. I could hardly leave them with the cook or with Mr. Albertson."

"Will you be back tonight in time for dinner?"

"Oh, yes, I should hope so. The yardmen will be ready to quit long before then," Josephine Albertson added with a laugh. "I guess they could work without my being there to watch every move, but they always seem to have some question that I need to decide. Since you're here, I'm able to go with them."

"Well, have a nice day," Mary smiled, picking up her books and starting toward the school, where she knew her four students were waiting for her.

"You too," her friend said. "If the cook has any questions, just use your own judgment. And if some emergency should come up, send Harold to the cowboys' foreman at the bunkhouse. He ought to be able to give you any help you need."

Mary nodded. "Everything will be just fine."

"It's quite a responsibility to be left in charge of a five-thousand-acre estate," Mary thought, then laughed. "Not actually the whole five thousand acres, Silly!" her mind chided her. "The cowboys take care of the land and the herd of half-wild range cattle. But the children and the cook are under my care. That's five people. And if you consider the mules and the milch cows, the total comes to quite a few more lives. With Mr. Fredericks and the yardmen all gone today, those untamed cows are my responsibility."

She opened the school door and greeted the children, who were already in their places. The sounds of singing birds came through the open windows of the school. Every now and then they could hear the cows' deep mooing and lowing.

In order to keep the household well supplied with milk, cream, cheese, and other dairy products, the cowboys brought range cows that had just had calves to the barn. The nursing cows remained there a few months, then the men took them back to the rangelands and replaced them with other cows. Because the animals had little contact with people, they had to be tied when milked. At night they remained in a large barn, but during the day they roamed in large wire-fenced yards.

The morning passed quietly for Mary and her students. Since it was a bright, sunny day, the children seemed to do their lessons extra well in their eagerness to go outside to play. At last the clock hands told them it was time for recess, and they hurried out of the little school.

Mary stayed with the girls and played hopscotch, while Harold ran around the house to stretch his legs. In a moment he returned, so excited he could hardly talk. "Cows! The cows are out!" he shouted. "Miss Moore, the cows have jumped the fence and are stomping all over

The Ungrateful Cow

the flowers in the front yard."

"You stay here," she told the girls as she hurried after Harold. Rounding the corner of the house, she stopped short at the sight. Cows were racing through the flower beds, walking on the shrubbery, eating the grass—making havoc of the beautiful, well-kept front yard.

"What are we going to do? What are we going to do?" Harold asked, feeling responsibility as the only male left at home.

"The bunkhouse!" Mary cried. "Get your bicycle and ride as fast as you can to the bunkhouse. Tell the foreman to send some cowboys to round up those cattle and put them back in their pens."

Harold scurried off before she finished speaking. Mary went back to see where and *why* the animals had jumped the fence. She discovered that the mules had gotten into the cattle pens and had frightened the cows so much, they had bolted over the high fence. Then she saw something that made her face go white with terror. A large cow had failed to clear the fence, and it hung, head down, with its hind leg caught in the top strands of fence wire. Creeping a little closer, Mary tried to figure out what she should do.

Its leg hung over the top wire of the fence, and its hoof had caught on the second strand. The strong wires held tight to the post, suspending the cow so the top of its head just touched the ground. The leg dripped blood, and the animal moaned in pain. Moved more by sympathy than good judgment, Mary desperately wanted to help the injured creature. She turned to see the girls watching her, their faces pale with fright. "What are you going to do?" Laura whispered.

"I don't know. I just don't know," Mary answered. "But I've got to do something." Then she turned to see Harold, red-faced, racing toward them on his bike. He braked to a screeching stop. "Well, where are the cowboys?" Mary demanded. "Aren't they coming?"

The boy shook his head. "The foreman said, 'You tell that bossy, empty-headed young schoolmarm to mind her own silly business and let me take care of the cattle.'"

Mary glanced at the injured cow and then back at Harold. "What are the ones in front doing?" she asked with a sigh.

"Just eating the grass and chewing on the flowers."

"At least they haven't run away."

"The mules have gone back to their own yard," Lois shouted from a distance. "Maybe we could run and shoo the cows back where they belong."

"Maybe," Mary sighed. "Right now I've got to help this poor cow before it dies." She looked at the animal and back at the children. "Girls, I'd feel a lot better if you were back in the schoolhouse. You may stand in the doorway and watch."

Reluctantly they left, and she turned to Harold. "Go get me the wire cutters. Maybe I can cut the cow down." The boy ran off for the tool while she stood watching the animal. It groaned in pain, and Mary knew that every movement brought agony to the twisted leg.

The cow hung from the fence near the barn. Fifteen feet away, against the barn, grew a clump of five large eucalyptus trees. Mary backed up against the trees, waiting for the boy. The trees grew so tightly together and so close to the barn that it was impossible to step between them and the barn or to slip between their trunks.

Harold came running back and handed the cutters to his teacher. Approaching carefully, in case the cow should lunge in fright or pain, she snipped the top two wires of the fence. With a heavy thud the cow fell to the ground.

The Ungrateful Cow

Mary stepped back against the little shelter of trees, feeling proud of her deed. She watched as the cow lay moaning and panting on the ground, and she wondered whether the poor animal would die anyway. Finally it struggled to its feet and tested its hurt leg. It seemed OK, and Mary smiled with relief. The cow stood on all four feet, then glanced around as if searching for the source of its trouble. When it saw the teacher, it instantly lowered its head and charged, covering the fifteen feet between it and Mary in a flash.

Paralyzed with horror, Mary knew that she was going to die. It would be impossible to dart all the way around the row of trees to escape the animal. A dozen thoughts raced through her mind. "Will the cow grind me into the ground?" she wondered. "Or will it flatten me against the barn wall? Maybe the barn wall will give way, and it'll push me through the splinters and crush me inside the barn."

She hoped she was ready to die.

Then, as suddenly as if a barrier had materialized between the cow and Mary—as if an angel had stepped between them—the animal came to an abrupt halt. Hardly realizing what she was doing, Mary put out her arm and patted the cow's forelock.

At that moment the ranch foreman rode up on horseback with several of his hands following along behind him. He took one startled look at Mary stroking the injured animal standing inches in front of her and realized the danger she'd been in. Without a word he motioned to his men to get the cattle in the front yard. He lassoed the hurt cow and led her back to her yard.

Still shaking, Mary went back to the school and tried to resume classes as if nothing had happened. Fifteen minutes later Harold remarked to her, "Miss Moore, your face is still white!"

Mary and all the children laughed, and the color finally returned to her cheeks.

Lisey lifted the last armload of clothes into Mrs. Killian's small car, then turned to smile at the elderly lady. "I'm sorry my grandmother isn't here this afternoon. I'm afraid I may have forgotten something that she wanted to send to the Dorcas."

"That's all right if you have. Just bring it Sabbath," Mrs. Killian said. "I wouldn't have stopped by at all except that your place is on my way to the welfare center and your grandma had said she'd done some closet cleaning and had some things for us."

She looked at her watch. "I'm running late, as usual. Well, Lisey, I surely do thank you. You people must never wear out your clothes. These are so lovely, and the summer has really depleted our supplies."

"Oh, you're welcome." She closed Mrs. Killian's car door. "I'll have Grandma call you."

"Please do. Good-bye now."

"I've got another story for you," Grandma told Lisey that evening. "That is, unless I've about worn you out."

"Not a chance. What's this one?"

"About Mrs. Killian. She hasn't always been a Seventh-day Adventist, you know. In fact, when her mother decided to join, Mrs. Killian just about had a spell. She thought her mother had flipped out for sure."

Lisey giggled. "How old was she? Grown up?"

"Still in school, but a young lady, I'd say."

"All right tell me. I'll add it to my collection."

"She told us her story as we sat around mending clothes at the welfare center," Grandma began. "I'll try to tell it just the way she told us."

Chapter 14

Stalled

"The seventh day is holy.... The seventh day is the Sabbath.... Mom's out of her gourd.... She's lost her mind.... Saturday is the Sabbath.... The seventh..."

The Grand Canyon Limited, a dark dragon, raced through the Kansas flatlands, and each clack of its giant wheels tattooed the unwelcome refrain into my mind.

I looked over at Gracie, my sister, her face paled by the night-lights in the darkened coach. Sound asleep. I wanted to shake her, to scream. "How can you sleep?" I demanded silently. "Mother's destroying her life—our lives. And you sleep!"

Gracie stirred as if my silent shouts had touched her. She drew up her knees and snuggled into her pillow. I leaned my hot face against the cool black glass of the window. Such a feeling of timelessness—this riding a train at night. Before, I'd always enjoyed the sensation of being "in limbo," suspended in time and space.

But now!

"Mom, why?" My thoughts burst out in a moan, and I turned quickly to see if Gracie heard. Her lips parted, her breath was gentle. She was the essence of peacefulness.

"At least we're on our way home," I sighed. "Maybe when I see Mom, I can help her. And surely David isn't into this heresy, too. Between the two of us, we can straighten her out." I looked down at my hands—

clenched fists in my lap. "Relax," I told myself. "Go to sleep. You'll be in Texas soon."

It had started out uneventfully enough. Springtime, the bare trees wore the faint, fuzzy greenness that hinted of newborn leaves. I remembered how warm the sun felt on my bare arms—fantastic after a winter of scratchy wool sweaters and cold Texas rain.

I'd helped carry suitcases out to the new 1928 Dodge that Mother had just bought and felt a momentary wistfulness that I wasn't going too. But for months Gracie and I had planned the trip to our grandmother's, and we hated to call it off.

And after all, Mom needed a vacation. Dad had been sick for three years, and Mom had taken care of him all that time. She never said anything much about it to us kids, but we saw the lines around her eyes and her mouth deepen with worry and grief. I was glad David had convinced her that a leisurely vacation to Canada was just what she needed. Just a couple years older than I, he'd had to grow up in a hurry when Dad got sick, then died.

I closed my eyes against the darkness and watched Mother scurrying back into the house for a last-minute check.

"Come on, Mom," David had laughed. "You'll have lots of time to remember what you forgot once we're on our way."

She stood poised on the bottom porch step, the branches of the blooming redbud tree like a Japanese etching behind her.

"Oh, Mom, have you called Doctor Tippett and made arrangements for someone to teach your Sunday School class while you're gone? Oh, and to take over your youth fellowship meeting and your Ladies Aid?" I asked.

Her hand flew to her forehead. "Oh, my dear! Ruth, I

Stalled 121

have, but I forgot to tell him who'll take what." She turned. "David, just a minute."

He locked the trunk, then came back to wait with Gracie on the porch. I went back inside, listening as Mom talked to one of the prominent spokes in the big wheels that turned the biggest Protestant church in Dallas.

Mother hung up the telephone and turned, sparkling. "I tell you, Ruth, Doctor Tippett is one of the kindest, most understanding ministers we've ever had. Even his voice shows him as the Christian man that he is."

True. Absolutely right. The train's jolting jerked me back to reality. "If only I can get Mother to go see Doctor Tippett," I thought, "then everything will be all right. He'll explain about this Sabbath business, Doctor Tippett will." "Please, God," I prayed. "Help me to be able to convince Mom to go talk to him."

Well, Mom met us at the station, and we could see that the trip had done her a lot of good. Her worry lines had faded, and she was absolutely radiant.

"You look ten years younger," Gracie told her as we threw our bags into the back seat. "What was it? That clear Canada air?"

"I *feel* it," she declared. "This vacation was the best thing I've done in years. Oh, you should have seen the wild flowers along the highway. Like red carpets, the Indian blankets and paintbrushes. And the bluebonnets——"

"David all right?" I asked, by way of avoiding what was really on my mind.

"Fine. Of course he had to work today." She eased the Dodge around a sharp curve, toward the street where we lived. "He's good company on a trip," she mused. "Always cheerful, no matter what." She laughed. "Anyone else would have had a fit, stuck in Lincoln, Nebraska, for three whole days with just his old mother for company, but he was a doll."

"Mother, why on earth were you stuck in Lincoln?" I put in. "You didn't mention that."

"Oh, yes I did. On the phone. You never listen, Ruth," she scolded. "That's how we discovered the Seventh-day Adventist Church."

"Huh?"

"Wait till we get home so I can tell you all about it," she suggested. "I'll let you two get comfortable first. I know you're tired, sleeping on the train in those narrow seats."

"Oh, no, I slept just great," Gracie told her. That's my sister—always on top of everything.

"I didn't sleep ten minutes," I mumbled. But we were pulling into our driveway, and Gracie started getting all emotional about being home again; so they didn't even hear me.

I showered ("I always feel so sticky after spending a night *awake* on a train," I told them) and put on a skirt and an old blouse. Gracie was putting away her things, setting aside her dirty clothes when I went into her room.

"Now what are we going to do about Mother?" I whispered.

"Let her tell her side of the story," she returned. "Then talk to David tonight. Don't be hysterical," she added. "She'll get over it now that she's home and involved in all her church activities."

About then Mom called us for lunch, and we sat down at the white table in our big, sunny kitchen. "Looks good," I told her, picking up my sandwich. "Lemonade, too, with sugared slices on the glass. Hey, Mom, you're not always so fancy."

"I'm happy," she said simply. And we could tell. She was different. There was a depth, somehow, in her joy.

She sat down with us, took a bite of her sandwich, then talked while we listened. I finished my sandwich and chips long before she finished her story. Didn't taste a bite either, if you want to know the truth.

When she finally quit talking, I had nothing to say. I just had to get by myself and think over what she'd told us. So I said that I was tired and should unpack and maybe take a nap.

Mom looked at me for a long moment, and I thought she was going to say something more. But she didn't. Instead, she stood, picked up my dishes, brushed a kiss across my forehead, and suggested that I take a nap.

Lying across my bed, I went over her every word in my mind. Now you may think this sounds weird, but I do some of my best thinking in the twilight time of half-awake and half-asleep.

A warm breeze fluttered my white organdy curtains and drenched my room in the sweet scent of the gardenia outside my window. I seemed to float while thinking.

What had Mother said? Oh, yes. A lovely day to travel, the first day. The new car purred like a well-mannered kitten, and the miles rolled by. They stopped at an Indian trading post in Oklahoma, ate their homemade lunch in a park, and decided to make a long day of it and spend the first night in Lincoln, Nebraska.

They got up fairly early the next morning, ate oatmeal with real cream—an unheard of treat for Mother—in the hotel coffee shop. Then she'd waited in the car while David brought out their luggage.

The car growled to a start. David put it into gear, and it wouldn't move.

David checked every part under the hood that he

recognized, but he couldn't figure out anything, and the complexity of it all simply confounded Mom. He wondered if something was wrong with the gears, but they couldn't imagine what. After all, it was a brand-new car.

So they waited till a garage opened, and then they called someone to come look it over. The man tapped and listened and examined all the wires and gadgets, then he announced that it was a bit of a problem. Somehow they'd stripped the gears. Unfortunately, they'd have to get parts from the Dodge center across town. But they were not to worry, as that wouldn't take but an hour longer.

I could imagine her sitting there, maybe rummaging through her bag and getting out her crocheting to pass the time. At noon the mechanic, the essence of apology, came to them. The small problem had turned into a big, hairy monster.

Since the missing parts were for a spanking new car, the Dodge people in town didn't carry them, and they'd have to order from Chicago.

How long would that take?

I had to chuckle out loud, remembering Mom's imitation of the mechanic looking away and swallowing his words.

"Well, uh, ma'am. Three days."

"But now I know that God had a special plan for us," Mom had enthused, and I could feel myself tensing, remembering. "If we hadn't been forced to stay in Lincoln, well——"

With nothing to do and no wheels, they decided to make the best of their enforced visit and see as much of the town as they could. So that first night they'd just started out walking to look around when they were astounded to hear "Leaning on the Everlasting Arms" coming from a building.

"Well, you know me," Mother had said laughingly.

Yes, I knew Mom. She'd gotten all enthusiastic at the old hymn and had dragged poor David in with her. And she'd heard all sorts of strange things that only whetted her appetite for the next night. And the next. And knowing Mom, I knew she hated it when the car was fixed and they would have to spend their vacation traveling instead of cooped up in a hotel by day and going to church at night.

Christ is coming back—and soon, she'd learned. The world isn't going to get better and better. "Well, open your eyes and look around," she asserted. "Poor Doctor Tippett thinks that human nature will triumph in the end, that we'll all get together in peace. But the Bible doesn't teach that."

"Oh, Doctor Tippett, you've got to help me!" I thought.

"And when I realized the truth about the seventh-day Sabbath! . . . It's been in the Bible all the time, but I never knew it," she said, shaking her head. "Well, I just had to call you girls and tell you."

Tears stung my eyelids. What was Mother doing? I had to have time to think, to get out my Bible and study before confronting her, convincing her. As the oldest daughter, I felt responsible.

"But surely Doctor Tippett will have all the answers," I thought, clinging to that hope.

Mother was really excited and all for seeing him—the sooner the better. David too. He was actually on her side. They had some papers they'd been given at the meetings, and they wanted me to read them. But I didn't want to confuse myself before meeting with the minister. Maybe later.

The very next day we all trooped into his mahogany office. My heart pounded, for I felt as if the future of our whole family lay in his hands. Mother told him—in her sparkling way—what she'd learned. He listened politely, but as if a little bored.

It hurt me to look at Mom, her face flushed and young with excitement, so I concentrated on Doctor Tippett. He did pushups with his fingertips, studied the pattern in the carpet, then finally spoke. His voice was that of an indulgent father.

"Now, Mrs. Everett, I'm sorry these people have gotten you all confused, all worked up over nothing. You see, my dear, this has all been changed. Today, Bible scholars realize that while much of the Bible is inspired, most of it was written by well-intentioned men who were expressing their own hopes and dreams and views. You just don't worry yourself with these details."

He smiled. "After all, that's what we're paid to do."

Well, after working with Mom for ten years, Doctor Tippett should have known her and her stubborn streak. She didn't say much, just thanked him and said that maybe she needed to study a little more.

As for myself, I felt betrayed.

When we got home, I couldn't wait to get my hands on those pamphlets. I stayed up till midnight looking up every one of the texts. When I finished, I realized that if I was honest with myself, I had to admit that the Bible said everything Mom had told us.

Next day, good old Mom, who never let any grass grow under her feet, went back to see Doctor Tippett. She armed herself with her literature for fear she'd forget some of the texts she wanted to show him.

Well, she hardly got past her first sentence. When Doctor Tippett looked at the papers Mom gave him, his face blanched, then it turned as red as fall apples. He was absolutely livid.

His words came slowly and measured, out of some

hidden well of hatred we'd never known.

"Get out of here!" he ordered, and his finger stabbing toward the door shook with rage. "Never, never come back until you forget this nonsense."

We hunted up the local Adventist church the very next Sabbath. Mom was ready for baptism right then. I mean she heard, she read, she believed. David, Gracie, and I took a little longer—studying, searching, arguing with each other, until we all not only knew in our minds but believed with all our souls.

But Mom was patient—she knew we'd see it the Bible way—so we were all baptized together.